THE POWER OF VISION

THE REFLECTION OF YOUR FUTURE

Habakkuk 2:2-3 (The Message)

Full of Self, but Soul-Empty
And then God answered: "Write this.
Write what you see.
Write it out in big block letters
so that it can be read on the run.
This vision-message is a witness
Pointing to what's coming.
It aches for the coming—it can hardly wait!
And it doesn't lie.
If it seems slow in coming, wait.
It's on its way. It will come right on time.

Metashar Dillon

Order this book online at www.trafford.com
or email orders@trafford.com

Most Trafford titles are also available at major online book retailers.

Printed in the United States of America.

ISBN: 978-1-4269-4377-5 (sc)
ISBN: 978-1-4269-4378-2 (e)

*Our mission is to efficiently provide the world's finest, most comprehensive book publishing
service, enabling every author to experience success. To find out how to publish your book,
your way, and have it available worldwide, visit us online at www.trafford.com*

Trafford rev. 10/28/2010

 www.trafford.com

North America & international
toll-free: 1 888 232 4444 (USA & Canada)
phone: 250 383 6864 ♦ fax: 812 355 4082

Table of Contents

Dedication

To God, for your revelation knowledge and unbounded love for your people; In memory of my grandmothers and grandfathers for leaving a legacy in the earth; my mother for being such an inspiration to me and helping me to see my future; to my husband and children who continue to see their future as God has called it. Thank you.

Key Notes

Who should read this book?

For so long, many have struggled with our life's purpose, vision and calling. These struggles have led to lifelong regrets for not accomplishing our full potential. This book is intended to outline how we get divine insights (ideas, thoughts, and desires) from God, interpret and transforming these into tangible accomplishments. At the completion of this book, it is my hope that the reader will move out into the great dimension, reflection of tomorrow to accomplish all that you desire.

In this season, the Lord is awakening the destiny on the inside of his people. He has reminded us that the rain will fall on the unjust as well as the just. So don't wait on putting into motion that purpose He has shared with you, for it will soon come into being, even if not by you. Take action today.

The Kingdom of God is soon to return, and we will be set into the rightful place as we embrace the principles described in this book. This move of God is trying to bring the entire body to an oneness in Him. He desires that his people will have all things in common, and those old wells on the inside will come up and flow. Begin to dig new wells. These new wells will provide the abundance we need to advance the Kingdom of God and leave a legacy in the earth.

Habakkuk 2:2 (King James Version)
 2And the LORD answered me, and said, Write the vision, and make it plain upon tables, that he may run that readeth it.

Biography - Metashar Bankhead Dillon

Mrs. Metashar Bankhead Dillon is a nationally known prophet and prophetic teacher and ordained minister of God. She speaks regularly across the nation and world, transforming God's church and empowering the Body of Christ.

She has attended many training and educational platforms from the Broadcasting School of Connecticut, Los Angeles Trade and Technical Institute, The Contemporary School of Beauty, the Economic Development Leadership and Training, Training for the Cultivation of Women, Bank Boston/Gateway, University of Hartford Women's College Business Entrepreneurial and Technical Programs, and is a certified Grant Writing Specialist.

She is the president of Kingdom International Economic Development Corporation (KIEDC, www.KIEDC.com). KIEDC is a non-profit foundation formed that builds on a commitment to deliver socio-economic change that will bring hope to benefit all of humanity. In 2010 KIEDC held its kickoff of Boomin' 2010 event in Bushnell Park, Harford, Ct., which featured free and informational services for the people of Connecticut ranging from food donations to bank mortgage assistance.

She has visited many nations and countries serving in the humanitarian and giving capacities, a renowned public speaker, and a great community activist. Her most known strength is in the Prophetic ministry of God. She assists pastors and leaders around the nation in developing a sound prophetic ministry through that administering of prophetic training lessons delivered onsite and business entrepreneur coaching. She has been in business since the age of 18, and has counseled many leaders, businessman, and entrepreneurs on new beginning and directions from the Holy Spirit. The desire of Metashar's heart is for the people of God in all nations to be empowered and reach their God-impregnated capacity.

Contact Information:
Metashar Bankhead Dillon
12 Wind Road
East Hartford, Ct 06108
Email:
Metashar@yahoo.com
KingdomInternationalEconomicDev@KIEDC.com
www.KIEDC.com

When writing, please include prayer request and comments.

Acknowledgements

It is with a sincere heart and my love with appreciation that I give God the Glory. Thanks to my husband for helping to re-ignite the passion and zeal in my walk with God to complete this work. God's timing is perfect. We know that this work will bless the Body of Christ, and stir the coals of the fire for fulfilling the capacity that God had placed inside. Thanks for the encouragement from all.

CHAPTER 1 – A Reflection of The Past

As a child, the Lord will teach you how to pray, and in your faithfulness, you will mature. He will begin to unfold his hidden mysteries and treasures as you mature in the Lord's timing. As a child, I could remember back before I started grade school. I remember having dreams, and I would see things in the daylight, and night hours, things that I was not able to explain. As a little girl, I was able to understand that God had his hand on me.

I had a grandmother who the Lord used to help me with my early childhood enlightenment. As a child, I spoke to God often and I knew his promptings of the Holy Spirit. He would let me know different things that are going to happen to people, my family, the elements, and things that I could not explain in the world. My grandmother would wake up and know things that were going to happen during the day hours. She would talk about the things that also happened in the night hours, or things to come.

I later learned that these things are called spiritual things. She would always talk about the things, plots and plans that the enemy had against her family, and the different ones that came into the family, to try and bring destruction to their lives. She would also speak about how the Lord would always expose them and their evil works, and overthrow their assignment. Weeks before she went home to be with the Lord, God gave me a dream that he was getting ready to bring her home with him and although her body was old, her spirit man was still flowing in the spirit. She continued praying, prophesying over her family, and speaking words of wisdom until her final days.

The Lord showed me as a child that she had a prophetic gift. She would speak at times about the other family members who died in the Lord, about how they were waiting on her. This mighty prayer warrior, prophet of the Lord, left behind a legacy of the mantle of the Prophet, and a legacy for her family and generations to come. I knew as a child the gifts she possessed.

I gave my life to the Lord at the young age of 9. I will never forget my experiences during that time. I had very few people to talk about these experiences. Other children would tease me, and call me names and phrases like "you can see through walls". We called it premonitions, because we didn't know better about the spiritual things. The first thing he gave me was a prayer life where I would pray all night long and experience spiritual things. Having the knowledge or insight, foresight and a prayer life, I had firsthand teachings of the things of the spirit.

This spiritual journey with an effective prayer life allowed me to catch up with my divine purpose from God, which was revealed through prayers and God's word. Later in life, He set one of the most profound prophets to be my spiritual dad. He is still young and walking in a powerful anointing. Times and events happened in my life that God revealed, and as I grew in grace and maturity in the things of God, I began to deal in different spheres and dimensions (demonstration of power and authority). Hearing God in prayer and then executing his divine assignment in the earth realm is the rule of the day. Here are some examples of these real life experiences that I often reflect on.

ஒஒ ஒஒ

The Runner

Through maturity in prayer, God would give me more assignments. An example was his direction to change certain laws, expose high level wickedness in institutions and government. He would reveal the hearts of man and their diabolic assignments against his people. A specific example was the concern of a rapist on campus where I attended school. I prayed to God for him to reveal his face, and he did. The next day a man came to our department and looked in the window. I heard God say that he was the rapist, and my whole body shook. My first reaction was that no one would believe me, and how was I suppose to articulate the message that I now had knowledge of. I moved my seat, and went and told my instructor, but of course, he got away.

The next couple of days, I was entering into a guard area door and it was the same man with a hat on facing the bulletin board with his back facing me. Immediately, when I entered in the building and passed by him, that same feeling came over me. I heard God say that he was the same man that had been raping the women. He instructed me to go back outside and get the police officer, warn him about what I knew, and let the police officer know that if you don't catch him quickly, and not let him get a distance away. He is going to run, outrun you because he is a runner. He could run very fast. As the police approached him, he took off running and escaped, but was eventually apprehended on campus.

🙟🙝 🙟🙝

A Burned Victim

As life continued, many other notable supernatural occurrences happened to me. These things I share with you are just one in the life of a prophet. There was a season of praying and fasting for long extended times with the Lord. When I would come off the fasts, I prayed to God for him to interpret my experiences and give me new direction.

In one instance, the news came on television that an explosion had happened, and there was a fire that has sounded like an explosion in a housing project community. Two babies, had burned to death, and the young mother was in intensive care. Attending physicians said that she would be dead within 24 hours. Well it was the talk of town, and later to find out that it was the niece of my mother, my uncle's daughter.

We prayed and the Lord instructed me go to the hospital to stand in his stead; speak and declare his words that she will live, and for me to declare the works of God. The Lord instructed me not to look at their faces, or believe anything the doctors would say or what I would see. Just tell them that the God that I serve is going to work a miracle that man has not seen. You just do your job, what God instructs, and He is going to do the rest.

The only part of her body that was not burned was her mid stomach area, but the doctors took that area also to preserve it, so her whole body was not well. The doctors sought to classify me as a radical Christian with high hopes; telling the family that she was going to live, as a miracle for a testimony of God; they called in the social worker to please, instruct me to stop giving the family false hopes. No one had ever lived, with this much of the body burned. The infections killed them. The social worker, who was also a Christian, said to doctors, "...she just believes; you just do what you have to do, and she is going to keep on believing in her God."

Well, it was my biggest case up until then. I had to have a confrontation with the doctors, with God. You have to understand, I was just a representative; God's agent on Earth. Even when I saw the machines go off, I saw her turning for the worst. I had to bring my prayer life up and go deeper into that secret place, to be in God's presence for divine instructions, God's will and direction concerning the matter. She is still living to this day with skin grafts, everywhere but her face where God said no. He face remains untouched and as beautiful as ever. She has more children, and the plot that went out after her, God exposed it. All of the issues surrounding the explosion at her apartment would come to light. God restored all.

ഏ๏ 9๏

A Prayer for A Final Move of God

Back in 1999 when I began to minister throughout the land, the Lord began to share lots of things with me, and leaders in ministry through prayer. Locally, he began to show me the changing of the Guards; there were lots of men of old that were going to pass and He gave me the time table in which it was going to happen. This instance started at a prayer revival at one of the "Father's of the Gospel", who prayed for one more move of God before he died. He asked God to bring forth today, that which he experienced in the past. The Lord granted his blessing, and instructed me to tell church get ready and make things right, because he had two more months.

I saw all types of miracles, signs, and wonders take place in that prayer revival. People were blessed and they were willing and obedient to God. During the service, I saw leaders leaving prematurely, because they didn't believe God. He showed me that the bishop had been having heart issues, spiritual and natural. Two months later that Bishop died of a heart attack.

༄༅ ༄༅

The Little Man

My husband and I met in what was orchestrated by God. His arrival and my desire to stand fast on the promises of God yielded great benefits. After just deciding to spend some time together, I introduced him to my mentor that was visiting the area. During the meeting, while the three of us were riding in the car he replied "...what is this flame that I see between you,...this is more than a business relationship...who is this little boy that I see.." Confirmation of this little boy came from a praying mother, during a later conversation without a physical meeting. We discuss more details during or discussion on the art of listening, but safe to say, the little man (son) did arrive.

༄༅ ༄༅

Spiritual Warfare

I believe that the highest form of spiritual wickedness against God is in the court system. Plans and plots of men (people) are played out as the enemy uses them. A university story of my son when he was in college where he finds himself in the midst of this system tells me that my purpose as a prophetic servant of God is to stand up to an ultimate test.

The Lord gave me a dream early one Friday morning about my son, and gave me instruction concerning an event (an arrest) that was about to take place. "You son will be alright", He said, and continue to give me instructions that I would have to use right away. He revealed the plan and plot of the university police whose hearts and deeds were desperately wicked. This story was unfolded and ended up with full acquittal of all charges, but the impact of my son's life yet remains. I tried to warn the university officials of their ultimate outcome as they continued to make their evil plans.

While this event helped to shape my life, belief and trust in the delivering power of God, it exposed me to the ultimate level of spiritual wickedness in the land. A young man was terrorized, kicked out of school, and had his high athletic hopes destroyed while individuals who could do something stood idle and watched it all play out in the court system. The headlines of the news article the following day read: "Criminal Justice 101" in Savannah. I knew then that this system of justice, while seemingly fair and equitable, has a way of destroying lives. I knew that God would triumph because He told me so, and even this system, kingdom, is subject to Him.

This event thrust me into a place where I was forced to legislate and infiltrate in the realm of the spirit. God had me to warn everyone involved in this demonic plot and high level of wickedness, that their plan would not work, and that we would fight this case all the way to the Supreme Court if necessary. God would expose them and a federal investigation would ensue because of the ungodly behaviors as a result. "Whoever did not stand up for righteousness would lose their job within six months," was the message that I delivered. The leading officer, witness, would eventually lose his job with two months of the warning. Other officials involved would get replaced within two months.You will have your own stories as you remember these key points. Develop and implement a deeper prayer life. Learn to hear God's voice (The Art of Listening) through the many circumstances that you experience today. Listen for the clear instructions, according to his word, as it relates to his deep desire for his people. Move out on these instructions as He gives you direction. Do your part, and watch as God does his.

CHAPTER 2 – Stretching Beyond Elasticity – A Point of No Return

God is Stretching You. Let's get the baseline on a couple of principles. It requires 1) being open to what God is doing, stretching us to a point beyond recognition, 2) an ear for the word of God and what He is saying about a matter, and 3) some understanding of this vast realm of the spirit.

Isa 54:2 Enlarge the place of thy tent, and let them stretch forth the curtains of thine habitations: spare not, lengthen thy cords, and strengthen thy stakes; Isaiah 54 (Amplified Bible) 2 Enlarge the place of your tent, and let the curtains of your habitations be stretched out; spare not; lengthen your cords and strengthen your stakes.

(The Message) Isaiah 54
Spread Out! Think Big!
1-6 "Sing, barren woman, who has never had a baby.
Fill the air with song, you who've never experienced childbirth!

*You're ending up with far more children
than all those childbearing women." God says so!
"Clear lots of ground for your tents!
Make your tents large. Spread out! Think big!
Use plenty of rope,
drive the tent pegs deep.
You're going to need lots of elbow room
for your growing family.
You're going to take over whole nations;
you're going to resettle abandoned cities.
Don't be afraid—you're not going to be embarrassed.
Don't hold back—you're not going to come up short.*

What happens when an object or skin is stretched beyond its elastic limit? You can receive stretch marks when skin is stretched beyond its elastic capacities, like a pregnant woman. It is widely known and accepted in the engineering world that there is a limit, elastic limit, where tissues and metals can stretch to and resume the original resting state. In business, stretching your brand's elasticity requires extending your brand into related areas to add to additional customers and consumers, and create incremental revenue. But stretching beyond the elastic limit (yield strength) results in permanent deformation, or in business, a place where you have totally revamped your product and the current customer may or may not recognize you.

Similar to the above scientific analogy, God is pushing us to and beyond our elastic limit. When we are faced with his plan, vision, and capacity, we are stretched (transformed) into a shape where our closest childhood friends hardly recognize us. We become transformed not of this world, but of the spirit of God. To begin this ultimate re-shaping of our lives requires a special gift of listening to the mind and heart of God.

❧ ❧

The Art of Listening, Seeing and Thinking

Listen at what God is saying to us. Jeremiah 29:11Jeremiah 29:11 (King James Version) 11 For I know the thoughts that I think toward you, saith the LORD, thoughts of peace, and not of evil, to give you an expected end. Jeremiah 29:11 (The Message) 10-11This is God's Word on the subject: "As soon as Babylon's seventy years are up and not a day before, I'll show up and take care of you as I promised and bring you back home. I know what I'm doing. I have it all planned out—plans to take care of you, not abandon you, plans to give you the future you hope for. We must come to listen to God with our spiritual ear, for he is a spirit. God said in his word that there is nothing new under the sun, so it is important to understand what He is saying about a situation. The art of listening requires an ear for the word of God deep in our hearts that arise in the time of need. When we need to hear from God, we listen to what his word says about a situation. This also applies to seeing in the spirit. Our thoughts about a particular situation should then come in line with His will. This is an art, and requires meditation and practice.

❧ ❧

The Spirit World

Here are some commonly used guides for understanding the Spiritual Warfare and Prophetic Streams – Hearer and Seers; True prophets have the supernatural, imparted ability to hear the voice of the Holy Spirit and Speak God's mind or council. **Hearers** have the ability to hear and deliver the voice and mind of God; to edify, exhort, to comfort, direct, correct, destroy and wickedness, and to build up. These Hearers are often referred to as Prophets. **Seer** - Refers to seeing as in a vision. It refers to gazing, visually. It also refers to visual "Seeing" – either awake or asleep, insights, revelations, warnings, or prophecies. Born-again believers have two (2) sets of eyes/ears for the physical and spiritual worlds. (Reference; *The Seer*, by Jim W. Goll)

> *KJV 1Corinthians 15:44, 46*
> *1Corinthians 15:44 It is sown a natural body; it is raised a spiritual body. There is a natural body, and there is a spiritual body. And so it is written, The first man Adam was made a living soul; the last Adam [was made] a quickening spirit.*
> *1Cr 15:46 Howbeit that [was] not first which is spiritual, but that which is natural; and afterward that which is spiritual.*
>
> ***1 Corinthians 15:44-46 (Amplified Bible)***
> *44It is sown a natural (physical) body; it is raised a supernatural (a spiritual) body. [As surely as] there is a physical body, there is also a spiritual body.*
> *45Thus it is written, The first man Adam became a living being (an individual personality); the last Adam (Christ) became a life-giving Spirit [restoring the dead to life].*

46But it is not the spiritual life which came first, but the physical and then the spiritual.

Refer to the *Eyes of the heart (2 kings 6:15-17), insights into* the *Spiritual world*

2 Kings 6:15-17 (King James Version)
15And when the servant of the man of God was risen early, and gone forth, behold, an host compassed the city both with horses and chariots. And his servant said unto him, Alas, my master! how shall we do?
16And he answered, Fear not: for they that be with us are more than they that be with them.
17And Elisha prayed, and said, LORD, I pray thee, open his eyes, that he may see. And the LORD opened the eyes of the young man; and he saw: and, behold, the mountain was full of horses and chariots of fire round about Elisha.

ೲಲ ಲೲ

Prophetic Purpose

Purpose of Dreams and Visions anointing is to awaken the people of God to the spirit realm and to illuminate the truth, and can confirm the direction of God. Dream Types and Language are images generated while we sleep that we see. God uses dreams to communicate to people (the just and the unjust):

Matt 1:20; 24-25
Matthew 1:20 (King James Version)
20But while he thought on these things, behold, the angel of the LORD appeared unto him in a dream,

saying, Joseph, thou son of David, fear not to take unto thee Mary thy wife: for that which is conceived in her is of the Holy Ghost.
Matthew 1:20 (Amplified Bible)
20But as he was thinking this over, behold, an angel of the Lord appeared to him in a dream, saying, Joseph, descendant of David, do not be afraid to take Mary [as] your wife, for that which is conceived in her is of (from, out of) the Holy Spirit.

God spoke to Joseph (Matt 2:13-14, 2:19-21)

Matthew 2:13-14 (King James Version)
13 And when they were departed, behold, the angel of the Lord appeareth to Joseph in a dream, saying, Arise, and take the young child and his mother, and flee into Egypt, and be thou there until I bring thee word: for Herod will seek the young child to destroy him.
14 When he arose, he took the young child and his mother by night, and departed into Egypt:

19 But when Herod was dead, behold, an angel of the Lord appeared in a dream to Joseph in Egypt, 20Saying, Arise, and take the young child and his mother, and go into the land of Israel: for they are dead which sought the young child's life. 21 And he arose, and took the young child and his mother, and came into the land of Israel.

God speaks to Sinners – Pontius Pilate's Wife's dream "… have nothing to do with that man…" and consists of actions, colors, creatures, direction, names and numbers.

Matthew 27:19 (King James Version)
19 When he was set down on the judgment seat, his wife sent unto him, saying, Have thou nothing to do with that

just man: for I have suffered many things this day in a dream because of him.

Visions typically happen during the awakening state, in a trance-like state. John on Isle of Patmos, "...I was in the spirit on the Lord's Day..."

Revelations 1:9-10 King James Version
9 I John, who also am your brother, and companion in tribulation, and in the kingdom and patience of Jesus Christ, was in the isle that is called Patmos, for the word of God, and for the testimony of Jesus Christ.
10 I was in the Spirit on the Lord's day, and heard behind me a great voice, as of a trumpet,

Vision, in the literal sense, refers to the plan to meet the challenges of the day. Prov. 29:11 where there is no vision the people are unrestrained, but happy is He who keeps the law. Christians are people with vision. We should set goals or targets in front of eyes to gaze on; Set our sight on the Lord; and ...at His goals, press toward the goal for the prize of the upward calling.

Phil 3:13-15
Philippians 3:13-15 (King James Version)
13 Brethren, I count not myself to have apprehended: but this one thing I do, forgetting those things which are behind, and reaching forth unto those things which are before,
14 I press toward the mark for the prize of the high calling of God in Christ Jesus.

15 Let us therefore, as many as be perfect, be thus minded: and if in any thing ye be otherwise minded, God shall reveal even this unto you.

Philippians 3:13-15 (The Message)
Focused on the Goal
12-14 I'm not saying that I have this all together, that I have it made. But I am well on my way, reaching out for Christ, who has so wondrously reached out for me. Friends, don't get me wrong: By no means do I count myself an expert in all of this, but I've got my eye on the goal, where God is beckoning us onward—to Jesus. I'm off and running, and I'm not turning back.
15-16 So let's keep focused on that goal, those of us who want everything God has for us. If any of you have something else in mind, something less than total commitment, God will clear your blurred vision—you'll see it yet! Now that we're on the right track, let's stay on it.

Levels of visions include spiritual perception, pictorial vision, panoramic vision, dream (sleep Vision), audible messages, an appearance, divine sight, open heaven, trance, out-of-body, translation, heavenly visitations.

ᴓ℘ ℘ᴓ

Be Led by the Spirit of God

Filled and led by the spirit give us the power to defeat the enemy. It is only under the Lord's umbrella of protection that we are safe. Spiritual encounters must be clearly discerned as the physical body (at enmity against God) has a way of presenting contrary encounters (false visions, dreams and messages) to believers. There are 3 sources of Revelation:

1) Holy Spirit – 2 Peter 1:21

2 Peter 1:21 (King James Version)
21For the prophecy came not in old time by the will of man: but holy men of God spake as they were moved by the Holy Ghost.

2 Peter 1:21 (The Message)
19-21We couldn't be more sure of what we saw and heard—God's glory, God's voice. The prophetic Word was confirmed to us. You'll do well to keep focusing on it. It's the one light you have in a dark time as you wait for daybreak and the rising of the Morning Star in your hearts. The main thing to keep in mind here is that no prophecy of Scripture is a matter of private opinion. And why? Because it's not something concocted in the human heart. Prophecy resulted when the Holy Spirit prompted men and women to speak God's Word.

2) Human Spirit Soul Romans 8:7

KJV
Rom 8:7 because the carnal mind [is] enmity against God: for it is not subject to the law of God, neither indeed can be.

Amplified:
7 [That is] because the mind of the flesh [with its carnal thoughts and purposes] is hostile to God, for it does not submit itself to God's Law; indeed it cannot.

(The Message)
5-8Those who think they can do it on their own end up obsessed with measuring their own moral muscle

but never get around to exercising it in real life. Those who trust God's action in them find that God's Spirit is in them—living and breathing God! Obsession with self in these matters is a dead end; attention to God leads us out into the open, into a spacious, free life. Focusing on the self is the opposite of focusing on God. Anyone completely absorbed in self ignores God, ends up thinking more about self than God. That person ignores who God is and what he is doing. And God isn't pleased at being ignored.

3) Realm of Evil Spirits – Acts 16:16-18

Acts 16:16-18 (King James Version)
16 And it came to pass, as we went to prayer, a certain damsel possessed with a spirit of divination met us, which brought her masters much gain by soothsaying:
17The same followed Paul and us, and cried, saying, These men are the servants of the most high God, which show unto us the way of salvation.
18And this did she many days. But Paul, being grieved, turned and said to the spirit, I command thee in the name of Jesus Christ to come out of her. And he came out the same hour.

Acts 16:16-18 (The Message) - Beat Up and Thrown in Jail
16-18One day, on our way to the place of prayer, a slave girl ran into us. She was a psychic and, with her fortunetelling, made a lot of money for the people who owned her. She started following Paul around, calling everyone's attention to us by yelling out, "These men are working for the Most High God. They're laying out the road of salvation for you!" She did this for a number of days until Paul, finally fed up with her, turned and commanded the spirit that possessed her, "Out! In the

name of Jesus Christ, get out of her!" And it was gone, just like that.

A simple guide for judging spiritual encounters and judging revelatory encounters should include the following; am I regularly studying scriptures and reading my bible? Do I have an active prayer life? Am I seeking purity, cleansing, and holiness of my life? Am I a worshiping member of a local church or fellowship? Am I committed to only a few people who speak in my life? With these questions, we can perform and evaluate the sources of the revelation. These sources, whether from self, Satan, or God is described in the word of God. We need to examine these sources for their origin first, whether a Godly or worldly message, and its fruit. We must utilize the spirit of discernment.

ঔৣ৹ ৹ৣঔ

Find its origin 1 John 4:1-3

1 John 4
1Beloved, believe not every spirit, but try the spirits whether they are of God: because many false prophets are gone out into the world.
2Hereby know ye the Spirit of God: Every spirit that confesseth that Jesus Christ is come in the flesh is of God:
3And every spirit that confesseth not that Jesus Christ is come in the flesh is not of God: and this is that spirit of antichrist, whereof ye have heard that it should come; and even now already is it in the world.

1. Examine 1 John 4:5

1 John 4:4-5 (King James Version)
4 Ye are of God, little children, and have overcome them: because greater is he that is in you, than he that is in the world.
5 They are of the world: therefore speak they of the world, and the world heareth them.

2. Check its fruit

Galatians 5:22 KJV - But the fruit of the Spirit is love, joy, peace, longsuffering, gentleness, goodness, faith,
Galatians 5:22 (The Message)
22-23But what happens when we live God's way? He brings gifts into our lives, much the same way that fruit appears in an orchard—things like affection for others, exuberance about life, serenity. We develop a willingness to stick with things, a sense of compassion in the heart, and a conviction that a basic holiness permeates things and people. We find ourselves involved in loyal commitments, not needing to force our way in life, able to marshal and direct our energies wisely.

3. Discerning of Spirits

3. Discerning of Spirits – Discernment or distinguishing of Spirits goes beyond our natural abilities. It is a gift, a supernatural gift from God. We cannot earn it. The different spirits; The Holy Spirit, Good Angels, Fallen Angels, Demons or evil Spirits, The Human Spirit.

⚜⚜⚜

Angelic Visitations

There was a season from 1993 – 2006 that I commuted to my local church of fellowship where the Lord put me on post for 1) Monday noonday prayer, 2) Sunday, two services,

3) Wednesday/Friday services. During these commutes spending time with God in my car praying, I experienced many divine angelic visitations. Some of these encounters were not friendly, but God would always prevail. He taught me how to war in the spirit during the many hours and miles over these years.

❦

God cares for us all

One night, after a very powerful service while traveling with a dear friend of mine, Sister Kim, I saw an angel on the right side of the road. This angel was huge, and was donning what appeared to be a weapon of sort. As I came nearer to it, it disappeared. I peered in my rear view mirror and it was on the rear of my car. I felt the fire of God get hotter and hotter, and I began speaking in tongues. I said softly to Kim, "Did you see that what I just saw?" She said "yes, an angel was on the right side of the road, and now it is on the car". I immediately asked the Lord, "Why did you dispatch his angel to me?" He responded, "...for the warfare that I am preparing you for." Little to be known then, many future encounters of angels have been dispatched for specific purposes and battles to come. While it became clear to me later that this angel has always been with me, it was a messenger from God preparing me for more spiritual warfare encounters to come.

One day while on the road, I had an open vision of a tree falling in front of me. I was startled, but managed to maintain a safe driving posture. Next, a belt was hanging from the tree, then man hanging from the belt. He was contemplating suicide. The Lord revealed to me who this man was, and he was someone I knew. I immediately picked up the phone and called him and said these words, "...**don't do it, the Lord loves you and you are somebody great in God. The Lord is going to bring you into your destiny, and this is not the way.**" He asked me how did I know, and I said that the Lord showed it to me. He later confirmed being in his backyard, with a belt, contemplating suicide.

What God does (be it an angelic visitation or dreams/visions), and how he does it varies from one instance to the next. What is true of these encounters is that God exposes the plan of the enemy and sends messages of hope to his people. We have untold capacities inside of us to be aware of the spiritual world that God has ordained from the beginning. He will work within his laws to get this message of hope and love to his people so that these capacities can continue to be birthed into the earth. God chose me to be a vessel, and I chose to do his work. He reveals what he wants in varying degrees to His children.

☙ ❧

In The Presence of God – A personal testimony

I have spent some time with God, fasting and praying. During this particular experience, one July 4th holiday, I decided to forego some family time and just spend it with the Lord. I am forever grateful for this decision. While praying, a light shown on me so bright, I could only manage to stay on my knees. As I tried to gain my bearing, a peered upward to see feet made of brass. During this experience, I clearly heard God's voice and his direction for my life to preach the gospel. The wind of the Lord came in the room with a closed door and no windows. My life was changed forever.

Faith to see/hear is this realm comes by hearing. Fasting requires faith, faith to believe that God will honor the sacrifice with even more spiritual knowledge and that we are drawn into a deeper, trusting relationship. This faith comes by the word of God. These are essential elements in being open to what God is doing and revealing to us in this realm.

Rom 10:17 So then faith [cometh] by hearing, and hearing by the word of God.

Romans 10 (The Message) - "Does anyone care, God? Is anyone listening and believing a word of it?" The point is: Before you trust, you have to listen. But unless Christ's Word is preached, there's nothing to listen to.

಄ಲೆ ಲಿಲ಄

CHAPTER 3 – The Power of Vision – A Reflection of Your Future

He Will Be Known in the Gates

Many years ago, God spoke to me regarding my husband's arrival, and how I would know him. He spoke to me of the success in my ministry that would follow, and that he would be my covering. He described the arrival of him many years in advance. He gave me clues (without a face) that I would know that when he arrived. Some included: A man of prayer and after God's heart, he would be a world traveler, he would be known in the gates of the Middle East.

I had spent many years praying and fasting, while getting myself together for his arrival. Even the day that he showed up, God said to me, "…He is here". We spent years getting to know each other as friends before we were eventually married, but our paths crossed in a time that only God could have known.

The important message here was three-fold: 1) That waiting for God to fulfill his promise meant that I should prepare myself while waiting. Not that I needed to change my appearance, but to understand who God had ordained me to be. What was my purpose and destiny? What capacity had God called me to? What is the vision for my life, and what was I destined to accomplish in God, 2) the sign of his arrival was a signal of a new season of my life. Prepare for him to show up in time and space as it would be a trigger to the beginning and calling of our joint purpose in changing the world, and 3) God will get the glory then, now, and in the future.

Our ultimate backgrounds in business ownership, entrepreneurial endeavors were a match and we were joined at the hip. Our united desire to see God's people successful in all that we do became evident very early. We know that our purpose and destiny were aligned in time that would be like nothing we have seen to help empower and coach people with the Lord's insights. So I take pause and reflected on some of the key elements that will continue to shape our future. These elements are true reflections of our future together. Webster defines these elements as:

Purpose – the reason for which something exists or is done, made, used, etc.; an intended or desired result; end; aim; goal; determination; resoluteness; The subject in hand; the point at issue; Practical result, effect, or advantage: to act to good purpose. Pro 20:18 [Every] purpose is established by counsel: and with good advice make war. Ecc 3:17 I said in mine heart, God shall judge the righteous and the wicked: for [there is] a time there for every purpose and for every work.

Destiny - Something that is to happen or has happened to a particular person or thing; lot or fortune; the predetermined, usually inevitable or irresistible, course of events.

Reflection - to cast back (light, heat, sound, etc.) from a surface: The mirror reflected the light onto the wall; To give back or show an image of; mirror; Of an act or its result) to serve to cast or bring (credit, discredit, etc.) on its performer; To reproduce; show: followers reflecting the views of the leader.

Vision - Webster defines this as the act or power of sensing with the eyes; sight; The act or power of anticipating that which will or may come to be: prophetic vision; the vision of an entrepreneur; An experience in which a personage, thing, or event appears vividly or credibly to the mind, although not actually present, often under the influence of a divine or other agency: a heavenly messenger appearing in a vision.

I believe that purpose is chosen, and destiny is pre-determined by God. A "now-anointing" is moving. Believe in the Prophet and you shall prosper. Be in good health, even as your soul prospers. Your purpose is something that you chose. It is the reason by which something is done or used. It is an aim, or something you set out to do. Destiny – That which has been pre-determined by God that you will eventually catch up to. What is it that I am supposed to do?

God defines these same elements throughout his word as he revealed them to his prophets.

KJV
Acts 2:17 - And it shall come to pass in the last days, saith God, I will pour out of my Spirit upon all flesh: and your sons and your daughters shall prophesy, and your young men shall see visions, and your old men shall dream dreams. The Message Bible reads:

The Message – Acts 2:17
"In the Last Days," God says,
"I will pour out my Spirit
on every kind of people:
Your sons will prophesy,
also your daughters;
Your young men will see visions,
your old men dream dreams.
When the time comes,
I'll pour out my Spirit
On those who serve me, men and women both,
and they'll prophesy.
I'll set wonders in the sky above
and signs on the earth below,
Blood and fire and billowing smoke,
the sun turning black and the moon blood-red,
Before the Day of the Lord arrives,
the Day tremendous and marvelous;
And whoever calls out for help
to me, God, will be saved."

ༀ༄

Build Yourself Up
While you wait on God to orchestrate the fabric of our lives, build yourselves up. Understand what skills and knowledge that

you need to garner while you wait. Understand the capacity you have currently, and allow yourself to be stretched to a point that God can use you. This does not mean to destroy the wonderful creation that He has made, but rather, re-define your rules of engagement on how you attack problems for solutions. Reframe your thoughts, ideas and life's questions. Renew your mind. We need to continue to renew our minds to a place of submitting our talents to God for use in his Kingdom. Renew to the point that we are line up upon line, precept upon precept, in order to fulfill our destiny.

ക്ലൈ ഉപ്പ

God will give you what you need.

This is a High time for God and being in God. Have vision and put it in perspective to its place in God. Rev. 11:15 Kingdoms of Earth become the Kingdom of God, to possess the land. God says that if my people who are called by my name will humble themselves, turn from their wicked ways, and seek my face, I will heal their land (2 Chronicles 7:14). Know that all you need to fulfill, and that your destiny is in the hands of God. It is not until our will and his for our lives are the same that destiny and purpose converge. Expect God's unmerited favor. God's favor cannot be measured my man's standards of measurement. God said to me, "favor is not fair. It is not manipulated, nor is it calculated, but it is orchestrated by God." It is not orchestrated by your own hands. Be in God's position to receive. When you are in position, we come into full knowledge of his supernatural vision for our lives. The only one who can impregnate you with supernatural vision is God.

Don't get overly excited by preached messages that just seem to raise your spirits for a day, but ones that cause us to be transformed. After you finished shouting, look at where your feet are planted. Are you in the same place as you were 5 years ago? But rather, understand what God says: Upon this rock I will build my church. This Rock is the Kingdom message. We learned the Lord's Prayer early in life: Let thy Kingdom Come. Well, do we know what that means or what it look like when it comes?

What are you working on or toward? Is it for you or for the Kingdom? From the message that you last heard, are you transformed in any way closer to what a citizen of the Kingdom looks like? You must have a Kingdom mandate and vision, or it will not come to pass. Don't look out just for yourself, but for the people (Kingdom). Your efforts must be for God, his people, and his Kingdom. You will be fruitful, and your fruit will remain. No more "man building man's kingdom". You will know if you have the capacity when you produce fruit and it shall remain (Matt chapter 16.)

God is trying to take you to a new dimension. This is the dimension where you will spend time in the presence of God. Much like intercessors, we have to spend time with God to understand our assignment, purpose, and destiny. We must continue to check out your surroundings and the individuals who are connected to us for alignment with that purpose.

We must build our networks of people that understand the connection between purpose and destiny. Don't be afraid to get out of the boat and get into a boat with someone who can handle your full capacity. Ask God, "What is my assignment?" You will know because there is a three-fold manifestation: You, God, and the people around you (relationships). This dimension is the place of rapid acceleration into the new Kingdom, God's Kingdom to come.

cooe orao

Make the Paradigm Shift to Soul Winning

In all that you do, soul winning is at the heart of God. This paradigm shift gives us confident to win souls for the Kingdom and develop these individuals into their rightful place. We should have the courage to witness to all manner of people: Rich and poor, free and bond, etc., thus says the Lord. Business owners and entrepreneurs understand this principle. Be assigned to empower people, even if it with a word of encouragement. This season is changing the fabric of our lives with or without our consent. The global economic changes force us to re-think everything. We must avoid be thrust into a cast system: Rich vs. poor, people refuse to deal with the present and the future. For in God, his plan and purpose, there is no lack. Provisions for soul winning will come and must be a priority in all that you do.

If you want to change, tell God that I have evaluated my life's blueprint and I am in the same place that I was 5 years ago or worse. I am not where I desire to be in you. Allow him to help you re-write your blueprint in line with God's. Speak what God says, about your Future. How do you see yourself? If we talk about our present (or past) situation, we always digress into it. Give our future over to the Lord. Seek Godly counsel or coaches to reframe your plan for reaching your destiny.

Ephesians 3:20 Now unto him who is able to do. Now faith. This a now message, what we need, we need God to be God right now.

Prayer: Glory and praise to God for the outpouring of anointing, demonstration of power, all that we will do; let your Kingdom come; the gate of my life and my city be open to Him; reign; your throne is everlasting; you are a great King; let the people tremble, the earth be moved as we prepared your throne; let men be blessed, let God be God in this season in my life; let men know your mighty acts; let the Gospel be preached. I receive your kingdom because it is your pleasure to give it to me. Let the saints possess the kingdom; overthrow wicked kingdoms; let the word of God have full reign. We lift up our hands to a Holy place to receive the receptacle of God.

The Apostolic and Prophetic draws people because of it leadership, direction, and God ordained power. What is this end-time apostolic/prophetic move of God? God is pouring out the latter day rain on his people. He said that old men would get dreams and young men would get vision. He is revealing to man by his spirit, His kingdom that is to come. We have prayed so many times, "…let your kingdom come…" Grab a hold of this vision, the one that causes people to be drawn to you. Promote it in your families. Develop a personal (spiritual and financial) roadmap for your family, church, community and nation. Our communities are suffering from the disconnect between our values and principles of God. We must understand that this is how we impact our nation and the world. We must become apostolic and prophetic agents for God to usher in his kingdom and its mandates. Our life's purpose starts at home with sound families and spreads throughout our communities and land.

Does your family have a spiritual and financial roadmap? Spend time in setting it up where each member is engaged. Establish clear milestones for the family. Make your future as physically tangible as you can. Create small enough milestones that the whole family can visualize and help to bring it into a reality. Celebrate the successes. In certain cultures, the coming of age is a planned celebration where the child is formally recognized as an adult. It represents a clear milestone of development. Is there a spiritual plan that you can articulate to your family on how to walk in the spirit? Do you anticipate the spiritual needs of your family, and are adapting to a changing economic world? As our country's value system degrades, do you have a clear value statement that you family works to and honor? Have you prayed, fasted, for the true purpose, destiny and legacy for your family? Is this a thought or conversation, or is it written? Do you know the strengths and weaknesses and threats to your family? All of these questions are intended for you to begin seeing, reflecting on your future. As you pray and find answers to these questions, God give you a glimpse of your future. Record it. Make it plain. Make sure you family understand it and can help implement it.

Do you know your neighbors; are you meeting with them and developing strategies for your street and neighborhood? Are you in constant watch of your surroundings to see the family next to you struggling to make ends meet? Does your neighborhood have a mandate to watch (or notice) foreign elements trying to infiltrate the walls of your kingdom (neighborhood)? Are you sensitive to the spies being sent out by the enemy to seek out the week elements of your Kingdom? Do you know the strengths, weaknesses and threats to your community?

Is your church actively developing a roadmap for its mission, vision for your community, nation, and world? "LET YOUR KINGDOM COME," you say! When his Kingdom comes, what will it look like and what part will your local church play in it? Are you actively defining the elements (peace, joy, and abundant life) of this kingdom and educating the members? if we are not aligned with one purpose for ushering in this kingdom, we cannot begin to articulate it to the world at large. Fortune 500 companies have led this challenge in defining their mission, vision for its employees. Many companies have thousands of employees and manage to successfully encourage and motivate its employees. Our national government, and lawmakers, does a pretty good job in identifying the challenges at hand on the stage of world leadership. But the kingdom of man, its local church has dulled out the senses of this end time, apostolic move of God. Do you know the strengths and weaknesses and threats to your church? What battle is your church engaged in?

The time has come for you to create the future you desire and see yourself in it. Your present thoughts and actions today will have some impact on your future and the legacy that will be created. When the Kingdom of God is in its full majesty and glory, a young child in the kingdom will be able to understand his purpose and plan that God has ordained before the beginning of time. The kingdom citizens operate with the full knowledge of all it benefits.

Look at some of these words described in Psalms: Psalm 103:1 Bless the LORD, O my soul: and all that is within me, [bless] his holy name. 2 Bless the LORD, O my soul, and forget not all his benefits: 3 Who forgiveth all thine iniquities; who healeth all thy diseases; 4 Who redeemeth thy life from destruction; who crowneth thee with loving kindness and tender mercies; 5 Who satisfieth thy mouth with good [things; so that] thy youth is renewed like the eagle's.

> Psalm 103:1-5 (The Message)
> A David Psalm
> 1-2 O my soul, bless God. From head to toe, I'll bless his holy name!
> O my soul, bless God,
> Don't forget a single blessing!
> 3-5 He forgives your sins—every one.
> He heals your diseases—every one.
> He redeems you from hell—saves your life!

He crowns you with love and mercy—a paradise crown.
He wraps you in goodness—beauty eternal.
He renews your youth—you're always young in his presence.

Psalm 68:19 (King James Version) 19Blessed be the Lord, who daily loadeth us with benefits, even the God of our salvation. Selah.

Psalms 68: 19 Message
19-23 Blessed be the Lord—
day after day he carries us along.
He's our Savior, our God, oh yes!
He's God-for-us, he's God-who-saves-us.
Lord God knows all
death's ins and outs.
What's more, he made heads roll,
split the skulls of the enemy
As he marched out of heaven,
saying, "I tied up the Dragon in knots,
put a muzzle on the Deep Blue Sea."
You can wade through your enemies' blood,
and your dogs taste of your enemies from your boots.

It is estimated that there are more that 50 million evangelical Christians in America. We assemble ourselves most every Sunday (and often during the week) to re-affirm our local churches' existence. In this new kingdom, we are so interconnected with our other community churches one cannot fall for the other. Communication and interconnectivity is the rule of the day. There are watchmen, intercessors on post 24 hours per day. We are united to further the Kingdom of God.

We are our brother's (and sister's) keeper. We stand united against all threats to our communities. Our walls will become impenetrable by foreign agents. We are united, not because of numbers, but because of the same spirit that works with us. We are called to dedicate our lives to the up building of his kingdom, not our small domains. We are less concerned about our own organization, but rather to be a servant for the people. As leaders, we are to point the individuals in the direction of God, and how he sees them in the future. There are no 40 Million member corporations in existence today, but as the body of Christ, we are united because of his Spirit. Because of the spirit in us, this kingdom is not limited to the mere boundaries of our borders or numbers

We need to be a mirror everywhere we go. God anoints for service, but we must have clean hands. There is no good thing that God will withhold from you for them that love the Lord. This message is a change message that we cause people to look at their reflection of the future that God has for them. Help them to write the vision, and make it plain. Your purpose is determined by you, but your destiny is determined by God. Where is your multiplication? Reflect today through God's eyes on what you will look like tomorrow. What you look like today is not what you will look like tomorrow. The influence that you have through helping others find their way will have enormous impacts on them and you.

ॐ

Fabric of the Kingdom to Come

Everything he does, we can have the confidence that everything is in place to support his kingdom. For a quick glimpse, let's examine some of the kingdoms in existence today. Look at the financial and business kingdoms for instance. There are rules of engagement if you want to play. There are rules for competition, branding, and marketing that help the business differentiate itself from its competitors. In this arena, research and development is key to bringing new products to the market. Securing and growing your market share is vital to longevity. These rules are in existence and will remain. Our advantages as believers are the incredible insights and foreknowledge that are revealed to us through his spirit. It also includes the leveraging of the instant networks of businesses promoted and supporting the Kingdom. It is a network or association of entrepreneurs whose foundations are built around the principles of God and his son Jesus. It will be about making the biggest impact for the kingdom by causing each and every dollar to be spent in the kingdom multiple times. The Kingdom to come will have its fabric woven by competitiveness as well as integrity that leverages its massive size to create innovation as well as best value; it is about a brand of Kingdom principles that the world would look to for the sustainment of its kingdom. The fabric of this king will stretch far beyond the laws of this land.

Revelation 11:15 speaks of God's Kingdom will come, as the kingdoms of the earth will become the Kingdom's of God. We must continue to find a way to transform these earthly kingdoms into the Kingdom of God. How, you might say, do we transform the media (television, radio, and internet) into the medium for God? How do we ensure a free and independent media with Kingdom principles?

Revelation 11:15 (The Message)
The Last Trumpet Sounds
15-18The seventh Angel trumpeted. A crescendo of voices in Heaven sang out, The kingdom of the world is now the Kingdom of our God and his Messiah! He will rule forever and ever! The Twenty-four Elders seated before God on their thrones fell to their knees, worshiped, and sang, We thank you, O God, Sovereign-Strong, Who Is and Who Was. You took your great power and took over—reigned! The angry nations now get a taste of your anger.

1 John 3:2-3 (The Message)
But friends, that's exactly who we are: children of God. And that's only the beginning. Who knows how we'll end up! What we know is that when Christ is openly revealed, we'll see him—and in seeing him, become like him. All of us who look forward to his coming stay ready, with the glistening purity of Jesus' life as a model for our own.

Seek God concerning your life. Why am I here? You may choose to be a doctor, engineer, lawyer, but God is after your eyesight. Is your purpose and destiny in covenant with one another? Your purpose is the pathway to your success in the Kingdom. When you are wealthy, you have power, a voice. Who is listening to people with little wealth? Where is your influence? ANNOUNCEMENT: Change your thinking and position to receive the blessing of the Lord. God is re-positioning the church.

Prophetic vision is one that requires anticipation of that which will occur or come to be, vision of an entrepreneur. We cannot maximize it unless you operate in the things of God. The kingdoms of this world will come to naught. God said that He has given us Power to Get (Create) Wealth. Where is your power? Eph 20 says, the power that works within you. We must have the correct mindset. God said that we can speak and decree a thing into existence. God wants to stretch you today to and beyond you elastic limit. He stretched Paul. Joseph was stretched through living out his dreams and visions. Daniel was thrown into the Lion's den. Moses was stretched. Jesus was stretched. "Why have you forsaken me," he said.

KJV Job 2:28 "..pour out my spirit". Are your eyes open to who God wants you to do. What capacity has he called you to.

Message: "pour out on all kinds of people..." People that don't look like you. Men of old is due respect, but the power the Jesus got up with is the power for today. Your tongue, and conversation needs to changes.

John 9:4 Work the work, in the present capacity. Don't get complacent after getting a blessing.

When we go to heaven (spiritually) and get the goods from God through prayer, we are to come back to earth for his purpose. Even drug dealers have entrepreneurial spirits, but they serve the wrong god. Change your partners and you will have good success. God knew you from the beginning. So going to Him in prayer is the channel for us to know the deep things of God. Stretching to the elastic limit will allow tissues to resume its original form. Brand yourself. Stretching will increase the limit. Don't work for money, but let money begin working for you. He desires to shape the lives of those that know and love him along the same lines as that of Jesus. He followed up by giving us a specific destiny, and has pleasure in completing what he has started. All you have to do is let him.

Have confidence in God. The devil does not have the power you have been giving him. God will take the foolish thing and confound the wise (educated). Do you want God to be God? Let go of all of you. This is the time that the manifestation of God to be revealed in the earth. There is no good thing that he will withhold from us. God's vision has the power to create, the power to heal, the power to save.

Genesis 1 (Amplified Bible) - 1IN THE beginning God (prepared, formed, fashioned, and) created the heavens and the earth.(A)....26God said, Let Us [Father, Son, and Holy Spirit] make mankind in Our image, after Our likeness, and let them have complete authority over the fish of the sea, the birds of the air, the [tame] beasts, and over all of the earth, and over everything that creeps upon the earth.(D)

Deuteronomy 8:18 (King James Version) - 18But thou shalt remember the LORD thy God: for it is he that giveth thee power to get wealth, that he may establish his covenant which he sware unto thy fathers, as it is this day.

Deuteronomy 8:18 (Amplified Bible) – 18 But you shall [earnestly] remember the Lord your God, for it is He Who gives you power to get wealth, that He may establish His covenant which He swore to your fathers, as it is this day.

Deuteronomy 8:18 (The Message) - 17-18 If you start thinking to yourselves, "I did all this. And all by myself. I'm rich. It's all mine!"—well, think again. Remember that God, your God, gave you the strength to produce all this wealth so as to confirm the covenant that he promised to your ancestors—as it is today.

Luk 10:19 Behold, I give unto you power to tread on serpents and scorpions, and over all the power of the enemy: and nothing shall by any means hurt you.

Jhn 14:12 Verily, verily, I say unto you, He that believeth on me, the works that I do shall he do also; and greater [works] than these shall he do; because I go unto my Father.

೦ၔ ၔ೦

CHAPTER 4 – Working in our Current Capacity – Kingdoms of Earth

Proverbs 22:29

> *Proverbs 22:29 (Amplified Bible) - 29 Do you see a man diligent and skillful in his business? He will stand before kings; he will not stand before obscure men.*
>
> *Proverbs 22:29 (The Message) - 29 Observe people who are good at their work - skilled workers are always in demand and admired; they don't take a backseat to anyone.*
>
> *John 9:4 I must work the works of him that sent me, while it is day: the night cometh, when no man can work.*
>
> ***KJV** Rev 11:15 And the seventh angel sounded; and there were great voices in heaven, saying, **The kingdoms of***

this world are become [the kingdoms] of our Lord,
and of his Christ; and he shall reign for ever and ever.

Revelation 11:15 (Amplified Bible)
15 The seventh angel then blew [his] trumpet, and there were mighty voices in heaven, shouting, The dominion (kingdom, sovereignty, rule) of the world has now come into the possession and become the kingdom of our Lord and of His Christ (the Messiah), and He shall reign forever and ever (for the eternities of the eternities)!

KJV Est 9:29 *Then Esther the queen, the daughter of Abihail, and Mordecai the Jew, wrote with all authority, to confirm this second letter of Purim. Est 9:30 And he sent the letters unto all the Jews, to the hundred twenty and seven provinces of the kingdom of Ahasuerus, [with] words of peace and truth, Est 9:31 To confirm these days of Purim in their times [appointed], according as Mordecai the Jew and Esther the queen had enjoined them, and as they had decreed for themselves and for their seed, the matters of the fastings and their cry. Est 9:32 And the decree of Esther confirmed these matters of Purim; and it was written in the book.*

⚬⚭ ⚭⚬

What are the Kingdoms of this world, and how do I Fit?

The Webster dictionary defines a kingdom as, a realm or sphere of independent action or controls; a community or major territorial unit having a monarchical form of government. John saw (in the book of Revelations) a transfer from a world kingdom to the kingdom of God. It fell into the rule of off the body of Christ. What is most important here is the act of transfer of ownership from the world. You fit in your current capacity, so do work as you do it today. You are to use these talents for the Kingdom of God.

෨෪ଚ ଚ෪෨

What happens when your talent is not used in the Kingdom, and how does God view you?

God created us to achieve our fullest potential, and multiply our talents. God calls the person who was given a talent, and hid it, wicked and slothful. While some refer to the message described in Matt 25 (story of the talents) as money centric, they should not discount the fact that God requires excellence in all that we do, our with our skills. Hiding your talents from use in the Kingdom is wicked and slothful.

> **Mat 25:25** *And I was afraid, and went and hid thy talent in the earth: lo, [there] thou hast [that is] thine. Mat 25:26 His lord answered and said unto him, [Thou]* **wicked and slothful servant***, thou knewest that I reap where I sowed not, and gather where I have not strawed:*
> **Matthew 25:25-26 (The Message)**
> *24-25"The servant given one thousand said, 'Master, I know you have high standards and hate careless ways, that you demand the best and make no allowances for error. I was afraid I might disappoint you, so I found a good hiding place and secured your money. Here it is, safe and sound down to the last cent.'*
> *26-27"The master was furious. 'That's a terrible way to live! It's criminal to live cautiously like that! If you knew I was after the best, why did you do less than the least? The least you could have done would have been to*

47

invest the sum with the bankers, where at least I would have gotten a little interest.

ஃ௸ ௸ை

Using your talent in the Kingdom – Using the Insights from God

God's offer to us extends beyond our natural senses, and our own reasoning. In fact, supernatural insights are communicated (various prophetic streams) to give us the edge. We have this advantage. Wisdom is a gift. Knowledge is learned. Faith comes by hearing. But the transmission and recognition of his supernatural insights require years developing what I call the Art of Listening. Purpose this in your heart that your spiritual ears will be opened. . Devise a powerful guiding strategy, roadmap, and compelling vision to that end. This takes practice, journaling, etc., to get to know how God speaks to us concerning a matter, and his direction and solution to it.

God will reveal his heart and will in the secret place for his people. He used me to speak into the life of one young lady that I mentored and spoke about the greatness that was upon her. God showed me that her daughter would become a successful tennis player in a vision. I called her, as I have done on many occasions, to tell her what I had seen. It turned out that from a very young age to the age of 12, she had dreams of becoming a professional tennis player, and had documented this in a diary. She saw herself replacing the now current champion William sisters. Through our many years of contact, and relationship experiences, she took action regarding her daughter and her desire to become skilled at tennis. God is up to something. It dawned on her why the house that her family recently purchased came equipped with a tennis court. Time will prove out the final plan of God, but we wait to see how this message from God unfolds. Her daughter is well on her way to achieving her God-given capacity.

Jer 34:17 Therefore thus saith the LORD; Ye have not hearkened unto me, in proclaiming liberty, every one to his brother, and every man to his neighbor: behold, I proclaim a liberty for you, saith the LORD, to the sword, to the pestilence, and to the famine; and I will make **you to be removed into all the kingdoms of the earth**. What are some of these earthly kingdoms? Not in the physical earth, but the systems of the earth. Education, entertainment, sports, medicine, media, industry, judicial, political are some of these.

Let's take for example the educational kingdom. There are newly discovered learning techniques every day. New methods of teaching and learning are at our fingertips. So a person skilled in these new techniques can utilize, dual-use skills, to train individuals for the kingdom. We watched a recent article on Anwar al-Awlaki, a Muslim fugitive cleric utilizing this same principle for radical Jihadists.. He has been called the next Bin Laden, as he has harnessed the skills of education and training and put it to use. The Christmas day 2009 bombing suspect; the military officer shooting in the midwest are among his alleged trainees. The worlds system of education is so powerful, the new tools of learning, delivery, and persuasion are at it pinnacle. Coupled with the emotions and feelings, man has the ability to create havoc and chaos, or organization and progress in the world. As Kingdom citizens, we choose organizational progress. We must utilize these tools right away for the Kingdom advancement to create the organization and progress in the body that God requires.

The Judicial kingdom is yet another. There are countless examples that are being played out in our judicial systems. Issues range from immigration/naturalization of new born citizens, human rights, and more. Suffice to say that there is a place where these kingdoms need our oversight and values. Individuals currently engaged in the judicial systems are needed to fight for the continual existence of the body of Christ. We are being challenged on many fronts in the effort to quiet God's word and His commandments to us. We stand to suffer major blows to how we operate and exist without the help of individuals currently working in their capacity.

Where do you fit? The answer should be clearer. Where do you work, and what do you do? What skills have God placed in your hands? What is your sphere of influence?

God has promised us that we will have good success as we go through this birthing process; first of understanding what He has placed inside of your, allowing it to come to full term, and the development into full maturation. These skills will produce the abundance that you are in need of. Make it a relentless effort to first get an understanding of how you fit, and then apply these skills to the fullest. We often find ourselves is great spiritual warfare by not having this vision of our future and roadmap clearly defined; defined in a way that we can overcome the spiritual challenges in our lives. Overcoming spiritual warfare requires sound strategies, good council, and action. Wait on God, but go to work daily seeking God's wisdom on how you can be more effectively used in His Kingdom.

Proverbs 4:7 (King James Version) 7Wisdom is the principal thing; therefore get wisdom: and with all thy getting get understanding.
Proverbs 4:7 (The Message)
  3-9 When I was a boy at my father's knee,
  the pride and joy of my mother,
  He would sit me down and drill me:
  "Take this to heart. Do what I tell you—live!
  Sell everything and buy Wisdom! Forage for Understanding!
  Don't forget one word! Don't deviate an inch!
  Never walk away from Wisdom—she guards your life;
  love her—she keeps her eye on you.
  Above all and before all, do this: Get Wisdom!
  Write this at the top of your list: Get Understanding!
  Throw your arms around her—believe me, you won't regret it;
  never let her go—she'll make your life glorious.

Biblical Examples of how to use people's talents for the Kingdom:

Persona	Skill Trade	How Used in Bible	Reference
Jesus	Carpenter	Built the House of God	**Mar 6:3** Is not this the carpenter, the son of Mary, the brother of James, and Joses, and of Juda, and Simon? and are not his sisters here with us? And they were offended at him.
Disciples	Fishermen	Fisher of Men	**Mat 4:19** And he saith unto them, Follow me, and I will make you fishers of men.
David	Sheppard	King and Sheppard of Israel	**Psa 23:1** [[A Psalm of David.]] The LORD [is] my shepherd; I shall not want.
Lydia	Entrepreneur	Kingdom Financier	**Act 16:14** And a certain woman named Lydia, a seller of purple, of the city of Thyatira, which worshipped God, heard [us]: whose heart the Lord opened, that she attended unto the things which were spoken of Paul.
Moses	Egyptian Ruler	Israeli Leader	**Exd 4:18** And Moses went and returned to Jethro his father in law, and said unto him, Let me go, I pray thee, and return unto my brethren which [are] in Egypt, and see whether they be yet alive. And Jethro said to Moses, Go in peace.
Abraham	Farmer/Toiler	Father of Faith	**Gen 12:1** Now the LORD had said unto Abram, Get thee out of thy country, and from thy kindred, and from thy father's house, unto a land that I will shew thee:

There are many bible examples, but these should give you a sense of how God uses ordinary and extraordinary people in the world to make phenomenal changes in his Kingdom. I would be remiss if not to mention my husband here and how God has placed him in the forefront of a fortune 500 company in international business and development. I have seen how the Lord transformed his life over the past years to make significant stride for his company. But his gifts and talents were not just designed for the world and its kingdoms. He now understands and applies his gifts to help transform all that he is in touch within the kingdom, be it through ideas generation or an existing business, prioritizing businesses opportunities, or business plan development I have seen God stir up his gifts for His use. Now he is calling you to stir up yours.

Question: How do I transform the gifts and talents that God has placed in my hands for use in the Kingdom? How do I find my place in the kingdom? Does God have a spiritual road map for me? What do I need to change God? These questions have been in the face of the body for ages, and the source of spiritual warfare in the minds of the people. Overcome these battles through consistent application of faith, hope, action, good counsel and strategies.

ৡৎ ৡৡ

CHAPTER 5 – Plan to Action - Create a Compelling Vision

Vision That Works
- *Jam 2:20 But wilt thou know, O vain man, that faith without works is dead?*
- *Jam 2:26 For as the body without the spirit is dead, so faith without works is dead also.*
- *Jam 2:18 Yea, a man may say, Thou hast faith, and I have works: shew me thy faith without thy works, and I will shew thee my faith by my works.*

Vision for Jerusalem -
Dan 9:4 And I prayed unto the LORD my God, and made my confession, and said, O Lord, the great and dreadful God, keeping the covenant and mercy to them that love him, and to them that keep his commandments; Dan 9:5 We have sinned, and have committed iniquity, and have done wickedly, and have rebelled, even by departing from thy precepts and from thy judgments.

In this passage, Daniel prayed for the transgression against God for himself and the people. Confusion fell among the people as Israel had transgressed the law. Judgment was imminent. God spoke to Daniel of what was to come, because of the transgression, and show him how the Messiah would come to redeem his people. God made provision for forgiveness for his people. He even gave them time to work out their transgression. In our life, and local church, we are called to pray for the sins and transgression of the people. God is faithful, and gives us time to work things out. He sent his son to reconcile us, and we know that we can become full citizens again.

We have discussed how God impregnates, imputes, his vision in you. Sometimes this happens through various channels. Take for instance, the major accomplishments that you have made in your life, ones that you have no idea how you were able to do in your own strength. It may have felt as if the favor of God was on you. There were doors being opened, chance (god-ordained) encounters that brought you answers just in time. In these cases, you could not accomplish them on your own, but you had the faith to believe that he would answer. This is the subject of this chapter in which we intend to describe. Even without the "how to", we begin with the capacity that God places on the inside of us, integrate in the element of faith, believe in our hearts that it will come to past, and stand firm in his word. We create a compelling story, picture, or vision of the end result that God promised. Just wait for him to bring it to pass.

Hab 2:2 KJV - And the LORD answered me, and said, Write the vision, and make [it] plain upon tables, that he may run that readeth it.

Hab 2:2 (The Message) –

Full of Self, but Soul-Empty
 2-3And then God answered: "Write this.
 Write what you see.
Write it out in big block letters
 so that it can be read on the run.
This vision-message is a witness
 pointing to what's coming.
 It aches for the coming—it can hardly wait!
 And it doesn't lie.
If it seems slow in coming, wait.
 It's on its way. It will come right on time.

꧁ ꧂

Vast Wealth of Information and Knowledge

In a practical sense, I believe that wealth and prosperity is no accident but is created by design. What I intend to outline here is a practical approach to creating wealth you need to accomplish God's vision for you. I have lived with these principles for years and can be applied to every level of wealth you aspire to be. It is one that should be used and adhered to. More of these details could be found in the famous book, "The Richest Man in Babylon", whose timeless messages applies to us today. Be it a small/large business owner or the leader of a mega-church, your survival and prosperity growth depends on it. So the question is how do we get started on a path to prosperity. The urgency of change comes from your desire for the Kingdom of God to be evident in your life. These elements are peace, love, and prosperity. To have these, we must use all of the resources that are apparent and those that are not. What I mean is that the beginning of wisdom comes from understanding that God, who is of infinite intelligence, gives to his children an abundance of knowledge and information to create and command our future. Specifically, God requires us to walk after the spirit to become the Sons of God.

We must tap into this vast resource to get and make the unimaginable ideas and thoughts a reality in the Kingdom. Take for instance our ability to communicate face to face to anyone around the world in real time. This idea or thought was transmuted into the mind and heart of man. In this vast resource of infinite wisdom and mind of God are the solutions to your situation and problems (opportunities for God to show himself). He is ready to release these as we walk into the untapped resource. Have you every prayed, then suddenly you had a dream or a "hunch" of a new approach to solving a problem? God is transmuting new ideas and strategies to you. Don't just brush these off. Have you ever asked God for a solution, and saw an advertisement of a new product that fit perfectly? Have you ever had an idea that you knew would be revolutionary, delayed moving out on securing this idea in the marketplace, and eventually saw it being sold and offered to the public? As children of God, we get the insight and foresight of things to come. God said that nothing on earth would come to pass unless it would be revealed unto his prophets first. As we serve Him, and his son Jesus, we exist in this prophetic realm. (The revelations of Jesus Christ is the spirit of prophecy).

Thus, begin with the spiritual understanding of the massive energy God has stored up for us to help us create a compelling vision. Don't worry that you don't have all the answers, but know that God will pour out these answers to you liberally. You may have prayed in the past for solutions that took time, months/years/decades, for God to answer. But I pray that the "now", suddenly, anointing of God be released in your life through these words. Reframe your words (and questions for God) for specific solutions to specific problems. Use your words to describe what the solution looks like, and reflect, meditate, upon this regularly. Act! Here lies the abundance of new ideas and opportunities for God's greatness to be reflected in our lives. Seek first the Kingdom of God, and all its righteousness, and all these things will be added.

⊶⊙ℓ ℓⓒ⊷

Eliminate Excuses

So with the knowledge of the vast storehouses of God, there is no end to what he will reveal to you. As you read these words, recall what ideas he has already put into your spirit. Is it a new invention? Go patent it. Is it a solution for someone else's dilemma? Go share it, in the wisdom of God. Is it a new business or concept to revolutionize an old one? Get help in writing the business plan. **MIND** your own business!!! The message here is action, no more delays.

Here are some of the excuses that Moses used to convince God that he was not up for the job. But God knew that he was created just for this job.

Exodus 3: 10-11
10 Come now therefore, and I will send you to Pharaoh, that you may bring forth My people, the Israelites, out of Egypt. 11 And Moses said to God, [b] Who am I, that I should go to Pharaoh and bring the Israelites out of Egypt?

Exodus 4:10-16
10And Moses said to the Lord, O Lord, I am not eloquent or a man of words, neither before nor since You have spoken to Your servant; for I am slow of speech and have a heavy and awkward tongue. 11 And the Lord said to him, Who has made man's mouth? Or who makes the dumb, or the deaf, or the seeing, or the blind? Is it not I, the Lord? 12 Now therefore go, and I will be with your mouth and will teach you what you shall say. 13 And he said, Oh, my Lord, I pray You, send by the hand of [some other] whom You will [send]. 14 Then the anger of the Lord blazed against Moses; He said, Is there not Aaron your brother, the Levite? I know he can speak well. Also, he is coming out to meet you, and when he sees you, he will be overjoyed. 15 You must speak to him and put the words in his mouth; and I will be with your mouth and with his mouth and will teach you what you shall do. 16 He shall speak for you to the people, acting as a mouthpiece for you, and you shall be as God to him.

We see here that one of the most powerful Old Testament prophets lacked some self confidence. He was human, and so are you. What he did have was faith in God to move obstacles out of the way and provide the resources and talent to accomplish the mission. What do you see as challenges to your vision? What distraction have you intentionally (or unintentionally) placed in front of your mirror? Imagine these as nothing but dust or smears on your mirror. As you set out to clean up your vision and your reflection, ask God to remove away anything that is not like him. Is there anything too hard for God?

ᴓ℗ ℗ᴒ

Decision –

The evidence of a true decision to change is followed by actions. Often we decide to change our situation be it through the inspired word of God, or the desperation of a tragic event. Either inspiration or desperation is helpful catalysts for change. But what happens when you are not inspired or desperate enough to consider change? Look at what the bible says in:

> **Revelation 3:16:** *16 So, because you are lukewarm and neither cold nor hot, I will spew you out of My mouth!*
> **Message Bible**: *15-17"I know you inside and out, and find little to my liking. You're not cold, you're not hot— far better to be either cold or hot! You're stale. You're stagnant. You make me want to vomit. You brag, 'I'm rich, I've got it made, I need nothing from anyone,' oblivious that in fact you're a pitiful, blind beggar, threadbare and homeless.*

We see here that God is not interested in the status quo. He is interested in getting the most out of our lives and his creation. Look around. Are you a constant agent of change to the lives around you? Do you have a passion for your fellow man in making their lives better? What is the legacy that you plan, or will leave for the next generation?

ঙ্গীৎ ৯৫৩০

Faith That Works

Most of us have heard the expression "ACTIONS SPEAK LOUDER THAN WORDS" , and whether you agree or not decision and action plays a vital role in achieving greatness. Imagine if some of the brightest women and men in the world held their ideas to themselves and shared them with only a few people. Action in this sense is intended to describe the step that follows decision. You must have (or build) the faith necessary to carry out the mission whether you have decided to make the shifts necessary to change your future, or whether God has inspired you with new instructions. What is faith? Hebrews chapter gives us what faith is now. God asks us to rely on it, as without it, it is impossible to please him.

Here are some practical faith action steps to prioritize the numerous ideas and get started on this journey.

1. **Look for the need**. What God has done with you is create a unique element of His "Periodic Table of Elements" that only you are best served in complimenting the body. Shortfalls that you see

in your church or organization are voids that need filling. Often times, we label our brothers and sisters as rebellious when they offer different ideas from our own, but these individuals have added insights that should be embraced and used for the Kingdom. They will add experiences that could give us the edge we need. They add to the team's dynamics that should be utilized and viewed as valid solutions to the cause. View these voids as areas you can serve in your current capacity to sure up the body. Understand that these business ideas are voids in the marketplace to fill a niche or need.

2. **Start by collecting** all of the ideas that you have pondered over the years for other ways to create wealth. If it is ministry, where have you seen the shortfall of the faith that seems to give you the greatest heartburn? Is it the lack of brotherly love, or charity? These challenges are not unique but should be solve and share with the masses.

3. **Work in this capacity** with all of your heart and soul. As you exert energy in improving the marketplace or body at your local church, it will catch on. Find, or ask God for creative ways to market your new position or product. Get help. Communicate the vision of the new idea at every level or opportunity. Create a powerful alliance or network of like-minded individuals to continue to develop and promote it.

4. **Ensure that your position or product adds value.** If in the local church, it should be in line with the vision of the church. If it is in the market place, seek advice from experience individuals in this field. Look for ways to improve the product, cost to market, and differentiation to similar products. Reframe your view of the marketplace as necessary to institute new improvements. You are one idea (thought) away from changing your destiny. For leaders, embrace new and innovative ways to solve your problems.

You have prayed, so know that God will send the answer.

5. **Get expert help when you need it.** Not all problems are new problems in the big picture.

This is the faith that works. This is the faith that transforms the intangible idea into the tangible realities. One other point to mention here is the influence of the concept of time and time management. Be aware of the use of time, every decision to act, every milestone or goal should have your commitment on when see that it will be achieve. God has the best of the best stored for us.

ﮩﮩ

Legacies That Last

> *Proverbs 13:22 (Amplified Bible) – 22 A good man leaves an inheritance [of moral stability and goodness] to his children's children, and the wealth of the sinner [finds its way eventually] into the hands of the righteous, for whom it was laid up. –*

> *(The Message) – 13:22 A good life gets passed on to the grandchildren; ill-gotten wealth ends up with good people.*

> *KJV Deuteronomy 5:9 You shall not bow down to them or serve them; for I, the Lord your God, am a jealous God, visiting the iniquity of the fathers upon the children to the third and fourth generations of those who hate Me.*

A best conclusion to one's compelling vision is measured by its ability to influence the next generations (grandchildren). God wants your seed, and so does the enemy. You will leave a legacy. The question is: will it die after one generation, or fade as a freshly plucked flower? Will the next generation celebrate and remember you? We so often forget to document the life and legacy of our lives, and leave our children with a clear understanding of their lineage. We find ourselves asking, "Who am I, what is my purpose, what is my destiny?" The answers to these life-long questions are found in knowing more of the legacy left for us, and our challenge to sustain that legacy. Have you struggled with really defining your legacy? It is much easier for us to stand on the shoulders of the giants that have come before us, than for every generation to rediscover itself. We lose time and energy re-defining who we are because we lack the often unwritten information from our forefathers.

The bible was written to document God's plan for man from the beginning of time to the end. In Genesis, it describes the plan of God to create man, in his image and likeness. Throughout the 66 books, a written testament of this plan is played out through documented accounts of the lives of the saints, and their contributions to his plan. It describes countless challenges placed before man and how they overcame these challenges. God spoke to Abraham and told him of his legacy and that his seed would be greater than the sand on the shore and stars in the heavens (Gen. 27: 17). The bible speaks of many detailed accounts of the lives of his servants' accomplishments that we can read about and garner inspiration to overcome any obstacle in our lives.

How wonderful would it be for your children, and their children to read of your accomplishments and relate them to their struggles? How important is it to you that your lineage is not lost as many have been lost before you. What untold advantages will your children have from first understanding what you accomplished, how you accomplished it? What wisdom will they have as an advantage over other children/people around them? Most importantly, thefailures you endured and recovered from should be marked as learning experiences not to be repeated. For the bible says that the very iniquity that plagued you will be revisited to your children, and your children's children. Your legacy will help to identify these pitfalls. Your triumphs over addictions and drugs, your darkest days, are all learning experiences destined to be repeated by your children unless the vicious cycle is broken. Leave a legacy that will last or your seed will just have to figure it out on their own. Empower your next generation to stand on your shoulders and reach heights that you did not. Give them an advantage to overcoming the world and their path of accomplishments by leaving a written legacy that will last.

~&⁄©&⁄~

CHAPTER 6 – Achieving Greatness, A Roadmap For Sudden and Dramatic Shifts in Your Life

Heb 11: 3 - Through faith we understand that the **worlds were framed by the word of God,** so that things which are seen were not made of things which do appear.

Ps 145: 13 Thy kingdom [is] an everlasting kingdom and thy dominion [endureth] throughout all generations.

John 9:4 I must work the works of him that sent me, while it is day: the night cometh, when no man can work.

Rev 11:15 And the seventh angel sounded; and there were great voices in heaven, saying, **The kingdoms** of this world are become [the kingdoms] of our Lord, and of his Christ; and he shall reign for ever and ever.

Mat 16:19 And I will give unto thee the **keys of the kingdom** of heaven: and whatsoever thou shalt bind on earth shall be bound in heaven: and whatsoever thou shalt loose on earth shall be loosed in heaven.

In life, to create the kind of dramatic changes in our life, we need either inspiration or desperation or change. When either of these elements appear in our lives, it is that moment that we need to seize and awaken the giant capacity within, and to immediately command our resources to conquer any area of our lives. In God's word, often times, we see that these are the only times that people will take action on their destiny. In many of the examples in the bible, inspiration seems the rule of the day. Let me give you a couple of examples: The twelve disciples were inspired by Jesus, and continued his message and direction to what we know as the church today. Job was inspired (and admired) by God. He held to that inspiration, even in a time of desperation and received more than double for this trouble. Moses was inspired by God to lead his people out of bondage to a promised land. Abraham was inspired by God and is viewed by many Christians, Jews, and Arabs as the Father of Faith.

But these same individuals experienced desperation like many of us today. Job had his family and wealth taken away. Moses fled into the wilderness after slaying an Egyptian Guard. The disciples suffered major desperation through persecution and death. Abraham fought his way through the desperation of killing his son, knowing that God would provide in the end.

So, either through inspiration of desperation, the individuals achieved greatness by first knowing that God was on their side.... *Rom 8:31 What shall we then say to these things? If God [be] for us, who [can be] against us?* Even sometimes, we are inspired to do greatness, but challenges arise where we desperately need help, leadership, and guidance to achieve the greatness that we are all called to be.

Be inspired to greatness, set your Kingdom mindset in place, and make the case that God has called you to greatness and has equipped you already with gifts and talents, ideas and strategies, blessings and resources to accomplish all that He has for you. He has given us POWER to get wealth. The power is within you, for He has given it to us. He has provided many tools, keys, even words that are at our disposal to speak to the mountains (doubts, obstacles, struggles) that they be flattened and cast into the sea. I ask you to change your outlook today on your future. I want to stir up the Holy one within each of you to begin, decide today to change the rest of your life and the world around you. Now decision means action. You cannot convince me that you have truly decided, or made a decision until you take action.

Let's start by looking into your future. The Apostle John wrote: Jhn 9:4 I must work the works of him that sent me, while it is day: the night cometh, when no man can work. This passage refers to the useful time of our lives in general, i.e. the days of his life or the Season of Effectiveness. For these useful days will pass away; and what we will have to show for it? Will we have the legacy of Abraham, or will we be forgotten, only after our children fade from the face of the Earth?

ചരു ളൂം

The mind and heart of man

God looks at the heart and man. He knows that apart from him, his thoughts and deeds are wicked. Gen 6:5 And

GOD saw that the wickedness of man [was] great in the earth, and that every imagination of the thoughts of his heart [was] only evil continually. The motives of man is self serving, self preserving.

So when God refers to the mind/heart of man, the medical community refers to this as the cognitive functions of the brain. The heart of our being is a function of our ability of reason, evaluate our circumstances, and interpret the constant stimuli being downloaded into our brain. As a child, we learned how to interpret our world from our parents and guardians, and them from theirs. The ability to accurately manage their stimuli passed from generation to generation. The interpretation of stimuli, and sins, of our forefathers are passed along genealogical lines, to be repeated over and over. But God, through his son Jesus Christ, has provided a means to decouple our thoughts and minds from the world to a spiritual world so that we can see the world (and ourselves) as God sees it. Thus, the transformation of our mind (brain) from the carnal to the spiritually source of stimuli changes our early childhood (and worldly based) method of interpreting our world to one that Gods intended for us to reside in.

❧❧ ❧❧

Let God's Mind be in you.

Phl 2:5 Let this mind be in you, which was also in Christ Jesus. This mind refers to having understanding, being wise, to feel, to think, to judge what one's opinion is, or to be of the same mind, agreed together, cherish the same views, be harmonious. God wants us to think of and see ourselves as He does. If only we could see ourselves as God sees us. To describe this, some of the characteristics that how God sees us would require that we have to have a relationship with God, so that He can continually provide insights, direction, and a glimpses of his future. Act 28:27 For the heart of this people is waxed gross, and their ears are dull of hearing, and their eyes have they closed; lest they should see with [their] eyes, and hear with [their] ears, and understand with [their] heart, and should be converted, and I should heal them. Century after century, year after year, the church has dulled down our senses both in seeing and hearing from God. But in God's desired state for our lives, we have a clearer picture of what we shall be.

God is infinite in his abilities, and his true essence (His Spirit) lives within us. In our most intellectual, carnal state, we pale in comparison to Him. Our brightest doctors, scientist, educator, and businesswomen can't begin to scratch the surface of the dept of knowledge ready to be released to us through Him. But, the world's system has caused a dulling of our senses to the true essence of how he sees us. For us to see ourselves as God sees us, we have to utilize the keys to the Kingdom by 1) Coming into a deeper relationship with God, through fasting and praying (our primary means for communicating with God), 2) Exercise our faith - Hebrews 11, and 3) Seeking first the Kingdom of God.

If we are to let God's mind be in us, we must make a clear decision that requires massive, deterministic action on our part to get to know the mind and heart of God. It requires us to pursue Him like none other. Through our pursuit of Him, through our desire to enter into the Holy Places, we begin to take on the mind of God. We begin to understand the heart of God.

ഏരൂ ഉരൂ

God's Plan for you can be good to extra-ordinary, Good to Perfect -

Romans 12:1 beseech you therefore, brethren, by the mercies of God, that ye present your bodies a living sacrifice, holy, acceptable unto God, [which is] your reasonable service. *Rom 12:2 And be not conformed to this world: but be ye transformed by the renewing of your mind, that ye may prove what [is] that good, and acceptable, and perfect, will of God.* His Acceptable Will is well pleasing, acceptable. His Good Will is of good constitution or nature; Useful, salutary; Good, pleasant, agreeable, joyful, happy; His Perfect Will is brought to its end, finished; Wanting nothing necessary to completeness; Full grown, adult, of full age, mature.

For man to achieve the extra-ordinary, we must utilize the depth, breadth, and width of the Holy One that lives in us. We must know that God is a spirit, and that if we are to worship him, we must worship him in spirit and it truth. Who can know the mind of God? His word says that in 1Corinthians 1:27 But God hath chosen the foolish things of the world to confound the wise; and God hath chosen the weak things of the world to confound the things which are mighty; He declared in Isa 46:10 the end from the beginning, and from ancient times the things that are not yet done, saying, My counsel shall stand, and I will do all my pleasure. In his perfect will for our lives, we achieve greatness. We achieve the extraordinary. We must live to our full potential.

⁖⁙⁖ ⁙⁖⁙

God's Perfect will for us has a Vision and Direction

Hab 2:2 And the LORD answered me, and said, write the vision, and make it plain upon tables, that he may run that readeth it. Visions start out as invisible, intangible ideas. A vision is a divine revelation (or communication) from God. The worldwide satellite communications was a vision at one point that came to be a reality. The car we drive, the computers we use were all a thought in the minds of man. But for God's desired state for our lives, we must consult him. We must go to him in Prayer. We must spend some time the prophetic realms, Kingdoms of God.

Setting goals is the first step in turning the invisible into the visible. Again, the path to success requires massive, deterministic action on our part. Do you want a deeper relationship with God? Has he called you to be a financier? Hasn't he called you to feed his sheep? Where will the resources come from? Decide today, and take action toward your future and destiny. Don't live in the past, as your best days are ahead. He has given us the power to create wealth. From this wealth, we must use it to fulfill the Great Commission… Go ye into the entire world and preach the Gospel. Proverbs 29:18 – where there is no vision, the people are unrestrained, but happy are he who keeps the law. Look at the references where God gave his servants visions to sustain them. Elisha 2 Kings 2:29-12 – Chariots and horses of fire; Jacob Ladder (seeds as dust of the earth) Gen's 28:12-15; Zechariah – Zech 4:1-7 …Not by might nor by power, but by My Spirit,' says the lord of hosts. What are you O great Mountain? Before Zerabbabel you will become a plain; Daniel – Dan 7:2-4 vision by night, I was looking…I kept looking at the revival of evil, but kept looking for the response from God. Dan 7:9-14 God dominion is an everlasting dominion which will not pass away. And His kingdom is one which will not be destroyed.

ஒஃ ஃஒ

Road Map Elements To Greatness In God; His desired State for our Lives

2Pe 1:1-11 Simon Peter, a servant and an apostle of Jesus Christ, to them that have obtained like precious faith with us through the righteousness of God and our Saviour Jesus Christ: 2Pe 1:2 Grace and peace be multiplied unto you through the knowledge of God, and of Jesus our Lord, 2Pe 1:3 According as his divine power hath given unto us all things that [pertain] unto life and godliness, through the knowledge of him that hath called us to glory and virtue: 2Pe 1:4 Whereby are given unto us exceeding great and precious promises: that by these ye might be partakers of the divine nature, having escaped the corruption that is in the world through lust. 2Pe 1:5 And beside this, giving all diligence, add to your faith virtue; and to virtue knowledge; 6 And to knowledge temperance; and to temperance patience; and to patience godliness; 7 And to godliness brotherly kindness; and to brotherly kindness charity. 8 For if these things be in you, and abound, they make [you that ye shall] neither [be] barren nor unfruitful in the knowledge of our Lord Jesus Christ. 9 But he that lacketh these things is blind, and cannot see afar off, and hath forgotten that he was purged from his old sins. 10 Wherefore the rather, brethren, <u>give diligence to make your calling and election sure:</u> for if ye do these things, **ye shall never fall**: 11 For so an entrance shall be ministered unto you abundantly into the everlasting kingdom of our Lord and Saviour Jesus Christ. His roadmap elements are:

Faith: conviction of the truth of anything, belief; in the New Testament of a conviction or belief respecting man's relationship to God and divine things, generally with the included idea of trust and holy fervour born of faith and joined with it. Relating to God, this is the conviction that God exists and is the creator and ruler of all things, the provider and bestower of eternal salvation through Christ. It is the subject of thing hoped for and the evidence of things not seen.

Virtue: a virtuous course of thought, feeling and action, virtue, moral goodness.

Knowledge - knowledge signifies in general intelligence, understanding; moral wisdom, such as is seen in right living

Temperance: self-control (the virtue of one who masters his desires and passions, esp. his sensual appetites).

Patience: steadfastness, constancy, endurance

Godliness - reverence, respect, piety towards God; godliness

Brotherly Love - love of brothers or sisters, brotherly love

Charity - affection, good will, love, benevolence, brotherly love

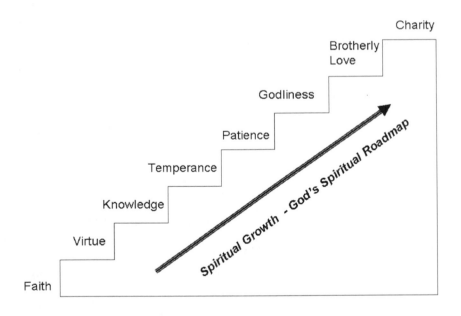

When we achieve and reside in the charitable state, we thrive in God's desired state for our lives.

❧❧ ❧❧

Two Prophetic Realms

There are multiple prophetic realms of God. In these realms, God is puroing out the abundance to meet our need. I will only cover two of these here, as there are the most tangible ones in use in our lives today. There is a prophetic relationship between spiritual and financial prosperity. This relationship helps us visualize the place where we should desire to be, God's desired state for our lives. This is the realm where God's spiritual desire for our lives is at its fullest and where we have the resources to implement the Great Commission. While there are no real hard lines for our existence, the relationship pictorialized below.

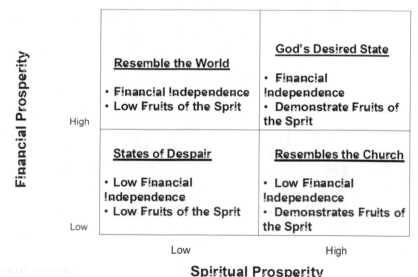

Quadrant I – Low Spiritual and Low Financial Prosperity

Financial - Negative Perception of Money, Negative Perception of the Church and its management of money, Lack of training on money management, Lacking money management experience outside of personal finances, Financial strains to manage day to day, At extreme risk to life events, No Financial Roadmap.

Spiritual - Lacking spiritual experience and application of Kingdom Principles and keys, Faith, Seed Time/Harvest Time, Giving, Receiving, Praying/Fasting, Binding/Loosing, Spiritual Warfare, Low Esteem relative to Fruit of the Spirit, (Love , Peace , Joy, Brotherly Love, Longsuffering, Gentleness, Goodness, Faith, Righteousness, Truth, Struggles in relationships and commitments, No Spiritual Roadmap.

Quadrant II – High Spiritual Awareness, Low esteem relative to financial prosperity

Financial - Similar to as Quadrant I, but understanding that God will provide all need and directions, Lacking money management experience outside of personal finances, at risk to life events

Spiritual - Developing spiritual experience and application of Kingdom Principles and keys, Faith, Seed Time/Harvest Time, Giving, Receiving, Praying/Fasting, Binding/Loosing, Spiritual Warfare, Developing Fruit of the Spirit, Love, Peace, Joy, Brotherly Love, Longsuffering, Gentleness, Goodness, Faith, Righteousness, Truth, Lightly defined spiritual roadmap, Able to sustain and honor relationships and commitments

Quadrant III – High Financial Awareness and Prosperity, Low Spiritual Awareness;

Financial - Reliance on Wealth, Self Reliant, Distorted perception of money, Negative Perception of the Church

Spiritual - Lacking spiritual experience and application of Kingdom Principles and keys, Low Esteem relative to

Fruits of the Spirit, Low/no desire to benefit the Kingdom advancement, No Spiritual Roadmap,

Quadrant IV – High Spiritual Awareness, High esteem relative to financial prosperity, Integrated Financial/Spiritual Prosperity, God's Perception of Money and its place in fulfilling the Great Commission, Can articulate and execute the purpose of the Church and its role in Kingdom Economics, Clearly defined Financial Roadmap, Integrate spiritual and economic Kingdom Principles and keys, Demonstration of the Fruit of the Spirit, Blessed to be a Blessing, Lender, Able to teach money management, Kingdom Economics to the Body , Articulate Spiritual/Economic Roadmaps, No Lack.

Spiritual and Financial intelligence is simply having a strategy for the Kingdom advancement. What area is God calling you to improve your position in Prophetic Realms? **This is God's desired state**. To increase in our learning; to be sensitive to his instructions for turning the lemons into abundance. It is not so much what happens, but how many different financial solutions you can think of to turn a challenges into millions. It is how creative you are in solving financial problems, and creating new revenue streams. We must understand the spiritual movement of God in his prophetic realms.

After your obligation to the Lord, Pay yourself first; master the art of self discipline. Without the discipline, money flows in the path of least resistance. This is a **cause of the poverty** spirit that is running throughout the body of Christ. Nice clothes, cars, house, and things are added as a result of seeking the

Kingdom. These things should not be sought after. But seek the advance of His Kingdom, invest money in place that will give a return, pay yourself first before the enemy comes to consume you mind and resources.

There are many spiritual laws of the Kingdom that has impacted our lives. They range form seed-time to harvest time, sowing to reaping, Faith, and more. But there are five that I can identify that have been most impactful to me. They are: **1)** Law of Prayer, **2)** Law of Fasting, **3)** The law of spiritual Warfare, **4)** Law of Miracles, and 5) Seed-time and Harvest time, and others. Knowing these laws help us to take on the mind of Christ.

⚬⚬⚬ ⚬⚬⚬

Seed-time and Harvest, a Business Initiative

This law is prevalent throughout the land, and most important to me. Whether Jew or Gentile, Christian on non-believer, the law of sowing and reaping is at work. As a business owner, I can recall countless opportunities that sacrifices have been made to sow more seed into the business through marketing. Also, there have been times where people have needed to get themselves put back together, but didn't have all the resources to do it. It often puzzles many that beginning with a purpose, or sowing the seed of what you desire to harvest. Through it all, if sow, you will reap. Marketing brings new and fresh clients. Helping individuals get through some tough times, establishes trusting relationships for life. The final key to this principle relies on the fact that we should not devour our harvest in total, but hold back a portion to honor God from with our first fruits, and a portion in preparation for the next harvest (investments). As the kernel fell to the ground and died, similarly, the sowing seems to be for naught. But on the contrary, the returns come back multiple folds.

God has established many laws for the Earth and the Kingdom. These laws are in place for us to occupy/subdue the Earth until He returns. It is to our best interest that we understand the true essence, apply, and live with these laws for us to get the most out of our Kingdom citizenship experience.

∽◍ ◍∾

In the Prophetic Realms Of God

God's desired state, there is high spiritual awareness, fruit of the spirit, your fruit remains, all need is met, financial resources are made available for God's Kingdom advancement. There is movement. When you are moving in God's desire plan/purpose for you to the desired state, he observes your every step. He orders your steps. He can send people, prophets (witnesses) to speak into your life, giving you the next glimpse and steps to the promises of God. He reveals the treasure, hidden treasure of God. The lack of movement in this realm causes frustration and stagnation. Abortion of your gifts and callings and the fruit of your loins occur.

∽◍ ◍∾

Sensitivity to the movement of God in this end time

Your next steps are just one network connection away and are passing you by because you are not prepared. God answers our prayers and we need to be sensitive to how He is moving. We don't put God in a box. They that wait upon the Lord shall renew their strength. They shall mount up with wings of an eagle. Waiting does not mean that we sit idly by, but it is an active place of participating and preparation in the next move of God. It means reading and developing new strategies, visions, business plans, business cases so that when the financier comes, he can read it and run with it, write the vision and make it plain. In the prophetic realm,

God gives us a reflection of our future, and brings it to pass in his timing. He can and will use the prophets to speak words of encouragement in our lives. But, there is no use for him to give you step 10 when you refuse to move off of step 0. He will withhold no good thing from us.

∽๑ ๑∼

There are enough provisions in this realm.

In his word, he declares that it is He that has given us the power to get wealth. He declares that the gold and the silver in the bowels of the earth, the cattle on the thousand hills is his. He awaits our awakening to create the strategies.

Let's Argue This Out Isaiah 1:19 (Message Bible)

18-20"Come. Sit down. Let's argue this out."

"If your sins are blood-red,
  they'll be snow-white.
If they're red like crimson,
  they'll be like wool.
If you'll willingly obey,
  you'll feast like kings.
But if you're willful and stubborn,
  you'll die like dogs."
That's right. God says so.

He wants our obedience so that he may divert the flow of wealth into your hands. In the prophetic realm, we have the mind of God in this realm. We know that we are more than a conqueror, our eyes and ears have not dulled to the movement of God, but as a sharp as that of the eagle. We can hear the gentle whisper of the Holy Spirit that we can ask the father, in the name of Jesus, anything and He will do it. We no longer are relegated to our old way of interpreting the world and events from our father and father's father. We can eliminate the generational curses of poverty, sickness and disease. They will not consume our seed. We can see the world as God sees it.

In the prophetic realm, God said that not one of His words will fall to the ground or return to him void.

Isaiah 55:11 says (amp) 11 So shall My word be that goes forth out of My mouth: it shall not return to Me void [without producing any effect, useless], but it shall accomplish that which I please and purpose, and it shall prosper in the thing for which I sent it.

Doing their work of making things grow and blossom, producing seed for farmers and food for the hungry, so will the words that come out of my mouth not come back empty-handed. They'll do the work I sent them to do, they'll complete the assignment I gave them.

In the Prophetic Realm, we can have the following assurances: **Expect changes to happen in our lives suddenly** (Acts 16:25-26 - 25 But about midnight, as Paul and Silas were praying and singing hymns of praise to God, and the [other] prisoners were listening to them, 26Suddenly there was a great earthquake, so that the very foundations of the prison were shaken; and at once all the doors were opened and everyone's shackles were unfastened.

Here is what we can expect:

1. Following your prayer and fasting, **miracles, signs and wonders will follow**

2. **Seed time and harvest time** applies to Sole winning and as harvesting the financial markets to further God's Kingdom

3. That no situation, ho matter how dire, is too hard for God (**is anything too hard for God?**)

4. **Kids grow up to obey their parents, and have long life**. We have the time, energy, and resources to train up the children in the way that God would have them to go, and they will not depart form you.

5. That **we can command the mountains** (sickness, disease, poverty spirits, debt, and lack to be removed and they are removed.

6. **Ask anything of the father in the name of Jesus**, and he will do it.

7. **Faith, (that come by hearing) is an action word**, and without works it is dead.

8. That we war after the spirit and that **we wrestle not against flesh and blood, but spiritual wickedness in high places**.

I pray today that the mind of Christ be in you, and that you change the way you view your circumstances and see them as God sees them. All things, good and bad, are working in our favor. God is faithful in illuminating the areas of our life that needs change. In the two prophetic realms, there is an integration of spiritual awareness and financial abundance that we advance God's Kingdom one dimension closure to that mighty day that he appears, and we shall appear like him. We pray:

- Walk after the spirit, and the righteous of the law be fulfilled – (Romans 8:1)
- Seek his kingdom first – Matt 6:33, and Luke 12:31
- Demonstrate the fruit of the spirit – Galatians 5:22
- Seek and define God's desire state (purpose) for our lives and family in the two spiritual and financial prophetic realms
- Faith is no longer a noun, but an action word (verb) – Heb 11
- Take on the mind of Christ – 1 Corinthians 2:16
- Our sons and daughters will prophesy and our words will not fall to the ground – Acts 2:17
- Act 4:30 By stretching forth thine hand to heal; and that signs and wonders may be done by the name Jesus. Signs and wonders will follow
- We sill speak healing and that they will recover, as Paul did

- Expect sudden changes to your current circumstances – as they did in Acts 2, with one accord.
- Ask in the name of Jesus - Jhn 14:13 And whatsoever ye shall ask in my name that will I do, that the Father may be glorified in the Son.
- Be sensitive to the movement of God in the Prophetic Realms of our lives
- Provision for his Kingdom advancement are ready for our getting, and there is more that enough
- We accomplish God's desired state for our lives.
- That we move into the next two levels of Grace: - Authority and Ability, and that Deuteronomy 8:18 (Amplified Bible), 18 But you shall [earnestly] remember the Lord your God, for it is He Who gives you power to get wealth, that He may establish His covenant which He swore to your fathers, as it is this day.
- Take action: Jam 2:26 For as the body without the spirit is dead, so faith without works is dead also.
    - Learn how to write an vision plan
    - Eliminate procrastination, no more
    - Develop our decision making skills
    - Beating procrastination, managing time
    - No more exuses

FATHER, in the NAME OF JESUS, we thank you for your inspiration for these messages. We pray that you open the eyes of your people to see, and ears to hear, and that as we move into your desired state for our lives, our divine purpose, sudden shifts will take place in our lives. Distribute your keys to your people today liberally. Let your Kingdom come, let your will be done today, O God. You ordained this day in time for the release of a new level of understanding the realms of your Kingdom. You give us reflections of our future. That in your

Kingdom according to revelation 11:15, the Kingdoms of this world are become the Kingdoms of our Lord, and of his Christ; and he shall reign for ever and ever.

Continue today God, in your movement to deliver your people. Unlock the mystery that you have held for this day, for we know that you will withhold no good thing from us; that as we continue to implement your kingdom principles, the keys to every door of your kingdom shall be opened and that we have free access to your citizenship, your true essence of abundant life, and your desired state for our lives. Cause your people oh God to begin to legislate in the realm of the spirit; cause your people to come into your presence and have manifestations in the earth realm in Jesus' name.

๛

CHAPTER 7 – God's Impregnated Capacity

1 Corinthians 2:12-14 (King James Version)

12 Now we have received, not the spirit of the world, but the spirit which is of God; that we might know the things that are freely given to us of God.

13 Which things also we speak, not in the words which man's wisdom teacheth, but which the Holy Ghost teacheth; comparing spiritual things with spiritual.

When you are properly equipped (and your birthing take place), it is going to cost you; you will have to be able to compare spiritual things with the Spirit. This cost may be money (investment) or time.

1 Corinthians 2:9-14 (King James Version)

9 But as it is written, Eye hath not seen, nor ear heard, neither have entered into the heart of man, the things which God hath prepared for them that love him.

10 But God hath revealed them unto us by his Spirit: for the Spirit searcheth all things, yea, the deep things of God.

11 For what man knoweth the things of a man, save the spirit of man which is in him? even so the things of God knoweth no man, but the Spirit of God.

12 Now we have received, not the spirit of the world, but the spirit which is of God; that we might know the things that are freely given to us of God.

13 Which things also we speak, not in the words which man's wisdom teacheth, but which the Holy Ghost teacheth; comparing spiritual things with spiritual.

14 But the natural man receiveth not the things of the Spirit of God: for they are foolishness unto him: neither can he know them, because they are spiritually discerned.

1 Corinthians 2:12-14 (The Message)

10-13 The Spirit, not content to sit around on the surface, dives into the depths of God, and brings out what God planned all along. Who ever knows what you're thinking and planning except you yourself? The same with God—except that he not only knows what he's thinking, but he lets us in on it. God offers a full report on the gifts of life and salvation that he is giving us. We don't have to rely on the world's guesses and opinions. We didn't learn this by reading books or going to school; we learned it from God, who taught us person-to-person through Jesus, and we're passing it on to you in the same firsthand, personal way.

14-16 The unspiritual self, just as it is by nature, can't receive the gifts of God's Spirit. There's no capacity for them. They seem like so much silliness. Spirit can be known only by spirit—God's Spirit and our spirits in open communion. Spiritually alive, we have access to everything God's Spirit is doing, and can't be judged by unspiritual critics. Isaiah's question, "Is there anyone around who knows God's Spirit, anyone who knows what he is doing?" has been answered: Christ knows, and we have Christ's Spirit.

We have Christ's Spirit in us. We have access to the things of God. We have direction communion with the creator of the universe. We have knowledge of his timing, his perfect time. Through this communion, we have access to the wealth, knowledge and wisdom of God. These elements are accessed by the spirit and are intangible (as the world describes it) in the beginning. Reach out. Grab a hold of this concept and we dive into the spirit realm. Learn of the spiritual nature of God. God is a spirit.

1 John 4:1 (King James Version)
*1Beloved, believe not every spirit, **but try the spirits** whether they are of God: because many false prophets are gone out into the world.*

1 John 4:1 (Amplified Bible)
*1BELOVED, **DO not put faith in every spirit**, but prove (test) the spirits to discover whether they proceed from God; for many false prophets have gone forth into the world.*

1 John 4:1 (The Message)
Don't Believe Everything You Hear
*1 My dear friends, **don't believe everything you hear.** Carefully weigh and examine what people tell you. Not everyone who talks about God comes from God. There are a lot of lying preachers loose in the world.*

Passion

One of the necessary things you must know is you have to have passion, which is something that is alien toward our nature, but you need it. It is a necessary tool. Passion is larger than your capacity. God impregnates you with purpose, and your passion to see it through will sustain. Either you have it, or you don't. Birthing the "God-impregnated Capacity" requires passion. This passion, or fire on the inside of you, is for God, His Kingdom, and His people. This capacity is not something you know how to do, but inspired by God. What you know is familiar; but what you don't know are the deep mysteries of God. This is something that you cannot handle on your own but inspired by God. To handle this capacity requires a whole **different level of FAITH**. We have to discuss how to we create and sustain passion.

Passion is bigger than you. Are you pregnant in your spirit that you don't seem to have the capacity for filling it? When God began to deal with you, it is not familiar to you. When God put something in you, your spirit, it is bigger than you because you need God to do it for you. If you can handle it, then you can manipulate it. If it is easy, then it is not God. But if God is in it, then you have to continue to ask God, step by step, and have (or develop) the right level of faith. We know that God has given it to us to do when we need God's help. You should not want something that is familiar; you want to search for the things bigger. Then, it can't be you. You need to stretch. You will always have success at what God is doing. I didn't say you won't have to battle, but you will have success.

Joshua 1:8 (King James Version)

*Jos 1:8 This book of the law shall not depart out of thy mouth; but thou shalt meditate therein day and night, that thou mayest observe to do according to all that is written therein: for then thou shalt make thy way prosperous, and then thou shalt have **good success.***

(The Message)

*Don't get off track, either left or right, so as to make sure you get to where you're going. And don't for a minute let this Book of The Revelation be out of mind. Ponder and meditate on it day and night, making sure you practice everything written in it. **Then you'll get where you're going; then you'll succeed.** Haven't I commanded you? Strength! Courage! Don't be timid; don't get discouraged. God, your God, is with you every step you take."*

*Romans 10:1Brethren, my heart's desire and prayer to God for Israel is, that they might be saved. 2 For I bear them record that they **have a zeal of God,** but not according to knowledge.*
Romans 10:1-2 (The Message)
Israel Reduced to Religion
1-3Believe me, friends, all I want for Israel is what's best for Israel: salvation, nothing less. I want it with all my heart and pray to God for it all the time. I readily admit that the Jews are impressively energetic regarding God—but they are doing everything exactly backward. They don't seem to realize that this

comprehensive setting-things-right that is salvation is God's business, and a most flourishing business it is. Right across the street they set up their own salvation shops and noisily hawk their wares. After all these years of refusing to really deal with God on his terms, insisting instead on making their own deals, they have nothing to show for it.

ोले 9ेल

Zeal

Zeal is another key thing every believer needs to understand in order to operate at maximal capacity. In fact, it will be virtually impossible for you to give birth to the Will of God for your life without the passion and zeal. This is a choice that we make, as God does not force our hand, but gives us a free will. If a birthmother gives up, and lacks the capacity, zeal and passion, to endure the gestation period, one of two things will happen; 1) Miscarriage (or abortion), or 2) premature birth.

In the case of miscarriage, the mother lacks the capacity (medical, will, etc.) to sustain the seed that is placed insider of her. In the case of abortion, the mother decides to terminate the seed. Either way, the will of God for your (your child's life) is limited to the gestation period. In the case of pre-mature birth, the child lacks the full development that is afforded by the 36-40 weeks of development in the womb. Some of the signs are under-developed lungs, the wind to sustain the body during this race. In either case, the true will of God is terminated, or under-developed. If this zeal is not present, expect undue challenge as you move from the birthing phase into the "Good Success" phase.

If you are not enthusiastic, start over. Zeal without understanding is not ministry. Without it, your ministry is at risk of termination (or abortion), or premature birth. You could lack the wind or capacity to endure.

Excitement but not understanding of the origin, or basis for your excitement can lead to error. Excitement without God intervention and direction will lead to failure. If God is not in it, it will crash. Your own motive is dangerous and at risk of coming against the plan of God. If you are excited about some idea, or revelation, try the spirit by the spirit of God. Seek counsel (Pro 24:6 For by wise counsel thou shalt make thy war: and in multitude of counselors there is safety.).

Well placed zeal as the ideal state for Good Success. It begins at conception and is sustained through Good Success (see Figure 1). Its passion is contagious. The lack of it is as lukewarm water (Rev 3:16 So then because thou art lukewarm, and neither cold nor hot, I will spew thee out of my mouth.). Do you know of people who exhibit these traits? Are they successful, or having Good Success? What do they look like? What do they eat (natural and spiritual)? How can you ignite the Zeal of God and have Good Success?

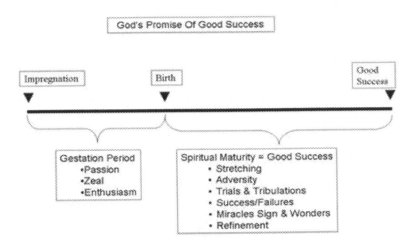

Consider these elements of some whom you know is having Good Success:

Time Table

This person is very conscious of the time table of God. A woman knows when she is impregnated, as her whole body changes, chemically altered, in a way of preparation. Having an idea of a timetable is always an indicator on how much fruit you will produce. What kind of fruit do you intend to produce? Is it the fruit of the Spirit (Gal 5:22 But the fruit of the Spirit is love, joy, peace, longsuffering, gentleness, goodness, faith)? Have an idea of the increase that God has called you to do. Signs will come if God is in it. Hebrew 10:27 (King James Version) But a certain fearful looking for of judgment and fiery indignation, which shall devour the adversaries.

Indignation

We must have a strong displeasure for things not of God. The thing not of God or his calling has to make you mad. You have to hate the demonic things (actions, words, and plots) that happen. (Rom 12:2 And be not conformed to this world: but be ye transformed by the renewing of your mind, that ye may prove what [is] that good, and acceptable, and perfect, will of God.).

Enabling Yourself and Others to Succeed

When you get along with everybody, it is not God! This is not to say or indicate that you should be disagreeable, but the contrary. We should agree with every word that comes from the word of God, and be an enabler of the furtherance of his Kingdom. We must seek after the Spirit of God and his direction. He is willing to pour out abundantly more that we can ask or think, not just for ourselves or our callings, but to the rest of the body as well. We should strive to be a more cohesive unit, community, kingdom that looks after our brothers and sisters. We should be sensitive of their struggles, and help bring the answer and resources to them. But we must understand that everyone does not speak the Word of God. In fact, if we don't transform ourselves and our thinking from how the world views it, we will become attuned to the distractions of the enemy and get the message wrong. If God gives you a dream, a vision, or speaks to you concerning a matter, ask him for confirmation and timing to release the message to our brothers and sisters. Conversely, if we don't seek after God's Kingdom and the enablement of his people, we become self centered and weighted with the cares of this world. Our light grows dim and are unable to function as effective as God needs us to be.

Something should quicken you spirit as the enemy begins to invade your camp. When God plants that seed inside of you, you should become sensitive to the enemies tactics to kill the seed, and that what God is imposing on you.

- Recall you're receiving a message, or prophetic utterance from God. Immediately, the enemy comes to convince you that the word was not "really" from God. He attacks the mind immediately. **Action:** Write it down in your journal as you received the word and immediately begin to fast/pray/war over this inspiration
- Everyday, the enemy desires to slow, delay, or eliminate that new seed that God has now impregnated. He desires to remind you of the old (untransformed) man that walks after the flesh. He constantly reminds you of your past to bring the flesh back to life. He comes to kill, steal and destroy your seed. Our routines have been so distorted with the cares of this world, and not the thing of God. **Action:** The old man is dead and not to be resurrected. Create a daily routine of commanding your morning. Daily confessions of your faith, and belief in what He has said will come to pass. You may recall how hard it was to transform your thinking. Look back only as a reflection of where God has brought you from.
- God is opening up the windows of heaven and creating the means and resources to bring it to pass. In his Kingdom, you have the authority by your

words to set a course for change. The enemy knows this principle but has caused many of the King's children to lose the confidence that God cares for you. **Action:** In your journal, record the speckles of light, glimmers of hope, confirmation from witnesses that he is sending your way. Never lose focus of your goal. These indications come in several forms. Some of these are dreams, visions, audible voices (tried by His Spirit), and confirmations from two or more witnesses. If you are skillful, you will hit the target.

To be an effective enabler, we should strive and develop good success habits. Some of the habits include, proper discipline, sharpening your skills and the development of strategies for success. These are some of the things that we can do on Earth as God imputes in us the strategies and insights from the throne. He promised that He would open up the windows of heaven and pour out blessing on us that we would not be able to receive. Start today by developing good success habits and paint the mental image of what you look like when it comes. Good sustainable success habits come from continual application of these principles.

Develop Proper Discipline

The consequences of good discipline is far reaching in mental, physical, and spiritual. Sound mental acumen requires the development of your spiritual gifts. As you go through life, you have learned to discern behaviors of people around you who mean you no good. We have made good decisions and bad decisions. The key here is to reflect on all these decisions, especially the bad ones, whose lessons were painful to bear. Their lessons are even painful to reflect on. But we must look at these decisions, their consequences and learn from them.

Get fit. The weight of God's glory is heavy. It requires long, extensive work habits and you begin to teach your young child to walk. You must develop good success habits not only to bear the weight of God's glory, but also the physical wear and tear on your body. With enthusiasm and zeal, it requires a substantial amount of physical endurance habits to get the job done. Apply the passion of good success habits to maintaining a healthy lifestyle.

Not enough can be said about seeking first the Kingdom of God, and its righteousness. God calls us to walk after the spirit to become the sons of God. Desire to know more of God and how he works. His spiritual nature is foreign to the natural man (world). He reveals himself to his children, but even then, we have to draw near to him. He is so gentle with us that He will not force himself or his will upon us. He desires that we make a concerted choice to seek and love him for who he is. Be determined, and passionate, about seeking God.

Develop a (your) skill

My mentor reminded me of these words: "Your skill will produce all that you are in need of". God has given to every man a measure of faith in him. Unfortunately, some chose to not recognize his existence. But for those who believe, God has added to each of us a unique place in his Kingdom. He has developed skills and talents in each of us. For some, these talents seem effortless in putting them into practice. For others, it requires constant learning, development, and sharpening of these skills to maximize your potential. Take for instance the story of the talents that Jesus spoke of. One servant took his talent and hid it (never sought to develop on increase his potential). For this servant, the master became very displeased. Don't let fear of failure inhibit your good success habits.

Be Disciplined To Learn – Wisdom is the principle thing. Wisdom is attained from God. We have to develop the proper environment within us for wisdom to take root and spring forth. Wisdom could be defined as having understanding, insight, knowledge, perception, astuteness, intelligence, and good judgement. Most importantly in the Kingdom, wisdom is in its best form when applied to life's challenges and achieving the best outcome. Ask God for wisdom, and see its application in every aspect of your life.

Heed instructions from God and his messengers.

Be careful who you entertain, as it may be an angel. As such, his messages and messengers come in many forms, shapes and sizes. In my life, I can account for many visitations from angels to deliver instructions or just be seen as a confirmation that God is with me. I can recount many instances where I would pass them on the highway traveling to and fro doing God's work. They have ridden on my vehicles, and protected me during accidents. They showed up often when I am ministering, usually in a strategic position, for me to recognize and deliver words from God. I recount seeing and rebuking the death angel on several occasions, in time for God's servants to prepare themselves. They stand guard ready to do God's bidding for us. The prophet Isaiah asked God to open the eyes of his servant to see them, and there were more of them working for us that there were working against us. You may or may not have the insights to see these beings, but know that they are there to do God's work. Their presence in our midst is God's way of telling us that He is an ever present help to us in time of impending danger. Heed the messages and the messengers.

Strategize

Learn the art to war.

Be Aware of Adversity

The enemy may send it your way to buffet you, but God intends to make you strong and make it for your good. Use it to your advantage.

Teach

Become so learned that you can teach the subject. While teaching, God pours out more inspirations and insights. Write in your journal of these things (inspiration and insights) often. God wants you to grow up. Adversity comes, not to overtake you, but to sharpen you and your skills. Consistent affirmation must come.

Train up a child. Don't tell children to shut up, but let them voice their opinion, but learning how to debate, they teach their children to ask questions. Don't beat them down, but build them up. Let them have a voice and be a part of the process. Help them develop the necessary tools. Because of the kingdom message, its citizen benefits, we must learn as little children. They add zeal and passion to our lives. They are the sustaining force that keeps us young.

> *Prov 22: 6*
>
> *Proverbs 22:6 (King James Version)*
> *6Train up a child in the way he should go: and when he is old, he will not depart from it.*
>
> *Proverbs 22:6 (The Message)*
> *6 Point your kids in the right direction—*
> *when they're old they won't be lost.*

You must be in the right place, not just church as usual, and in the right environment. You will be stretched and must get accustomed to moving out; you can't be stuck in a familiar place. Adversity puts you on your knees, but causes you to be in a place where you are assured to be able to hear from God.

⁓๑ᘒ ᘐ๑⁓

Conclusion

Time and Seasons are critical aspects in implementation of God's impregnated capacity. Words released in the earth realm must agree with God's plan and due season. I can recall a season that the Lord had me to release words into people's lives that would change their life forever. Sometimes these prophetic utterances would take years for them to come to pass.

God revealed to me some details about how the enemy would come against leaders in the Body of Christ, ten years prior. How do we remember, and keep track of the specifics. Well, this prophetic utterance was to a specific person whom I have been in touch with through the years as a powerful intercessor, " God will raise you up to change the economics and will be used as that weight and balance for the Body of Christ to set their finances in order." God would use her to be the point person in the recovery from this attack.

When the new article of the attack came, it triggered the event, that was spoken years ago. My words to her were, " get ready, they will be calling you." He would use her to fix others in the body of Christ around the world. We watched this unfold over a long period of time.

But God is accelerating the realization of the very utterance today, in real time. While before, we would journal, wait, and watch things come to pass. We still do these things today, but he is closing the gap between the spoken word and when it comes to pass. While the years of training has allowed me to speak into more of a now situation, God is fulfilling these same words not in the period of years, but of months and days. Not only will He reveal what he wants, but He will also bring it to pass when he wants.

What is different now is that we, the Body of Christ, have a deeper revelation of his word as we continue to grow into our relationship with him. However He does it, and when he does it, it does not relieve us of the task of making sure we do our part. While we wait on him, we are to prepare for time and the word to arrive at a point where they convergence. Let us subdue the kingdoms of this earth, prepare for the Kingdom of God to come. Let us accept God's plan and vision for our lives, receive the utterances sent to us by his prophets and reflect on our future in Him. Let God be God. Be Blessed.

The final event that I will talk to you about is for the business people who have struggled for solutions during these dramatic economic times. There is a man that prophesied to regarding his desperate attempt to find oil from the many countless hours of drilling and exhausting many millions of dollars in the process. In one simple utterance during time in prayer, the Lord showed me his hand, reach into the bowels of the earth and cause the oil to move and flow. His instructions were for the man to return to drilling, and in three days, what man could not do, the Lord would do it. He went to the wells on the third day, and the oil started flowing out of the earth. Obey his instructions, and you will be blessed.

Prayer: Father, in Jesus' name, we give you glory and honor and praise. Now we lift your name on high that you are Lord and over your people's lives and all power is in your hand; that every knee shall bow and every tongue shall confess that Jesus Christ is Lord. Even as the man/women need prayer and a word from you because they do not know which way to turn, use them as a symbol that as in

- Psalm 46:10 (King James Version) - Be still, and know that I am God: I will be exalted among the heathen, I will be exalted in the earth.

- Psalm 4:4 (King James Version) - Stand in awe, and sin not: commune with your own heart upon your bed, and be still. Selah.

I wait patiently for the Lord and He inclined unto me, and hear my cry, and that the resurrection power of God moved in our behalf. Let your manifest glory be released in their lives of your people to subdue the kingdoms of this earth. Cause the same power that resurrected Jesus to resurrect their situation and let them experience the fire of the Holy Ghost. Let them be filled with new wine. Awake them to come and live the lives that you have called them to. Cause a true reflection of their future to be revealed to them. Cause the old wells of our lives to come alive, and new wells to be drilled. Continue to stretch us up to and beyond the elastic limit where we move out into your perfect will for our lives. Impregnate us with your capacity to subdue kingdoms. Cause our past experiences to come alive and attest to the hand of God in our lives, and that we utilize the skills that God have give us in our current capacity for the Kingdom. Give us the Power of your vision for our future. Cause your end-time prophets to be trained to hear from you first, and to speak your words concerning the future lives of your people, and that the sudden winds of change will be evident in this 21st century. Let a suddenly anointing transcend in the land, and the changing of the new guards come forth and let them take their rightful place. In Jesus' name I pray.

Scriptural Food – For Daily Affirmations

1Cr 2:6 ¶ Howbeit we speak wisdom among them that are perfect: yet not the wisdom of this world, nor of the princes of this world, that come to nought:

1Cr 2:7 But we speak the wisdom of God in a mystery, [even] the hidden [wisdom], which God ordained before the world unto our glory:

1Cr 2:8 Which none of the princes of this world knew: for had they known [it], they would not have crucified the Lord of glory.

1Cr 2:9 But as it is written, Eye hath not seen, nor ear heard, neither have entered into the heart of man, the things which God hath prepared for them that love him.

1Cr 2:10 But God hath revealed [them] unto us by his Spirit: for the Spirit searcheth all things, yea, the deep things of God.

1Cr 2:11 For what man knoweth the things of a man, save the spirit of man which is in him? even so the things of God knoweth no man, but the Spirit of God.

1Cr 2:12 Now we have received, not the spirit of the world, but the spirit which is of God; that we might know the things that are freely given to us of God.

1Cr 2:13 Which things also we speak, not in the words which man's wisdom teacheth, but which the Holy Ghost teacheth; comparing spiritual things with spiritual.

1Cr 2:14 But the natural man receiveth not the things of the Spirit of God: for they are foolishness unto him: neither can he know [them], because they are spiritually discerned.

1Cr 2:15 But he that is spiritual judgeth all things, yet he himself is judged of no man.

1Cr 2:16 For who hath known the mind of the Lord, that he may instruct him? But we have the mind of Christ.

References:

Unless otherwise indicated, all scripture quotations are from the Holy Bible, New King James Version, © 1979, 1980, 1982 by Thomas Nelson, Inc., Nashville, Tennessee.

Scripture quotations marked KJV or King James Version are from the Authorized King James Version of the Bible and are in the public domain.

Scripture quotations marked Amplified, or (The) Message, are from the Bible Gateway (http://www.biblegateway.com/).

Webster Dictionary